SONGS FOR THE BATTLEFIELD

A Daily Devotional through the Psalms (1-75)

Charity Woon

Songs for the Battlefield

Copyright © 2018 by Charity Woon

Scripture within the text is taken from the King James Version of the Bible.

Contents

Dedication

To my oldest child and soldier, Benjamin, our favorite
Army Guy

Dear Son,

Words cannot express how proud I am of you. I
always told you I would forever be your biggest
cheerleader. I wish we could have attended your
graduation from Basic Combat Training. We always
knew our choice to follow the Lord to serve Him on
the mission field would sometimes cost us certain
privileges like attending special events. As a family
we understood that, and we were willing to follow His
lead anyway, trusting that He would bless us beyond
anything we ever felt we sacrificed. He truly has
blessed us far beyond measure.

We were thrilled to be able to watch the BCT
graduation live on the internet here in Asia. We had
no doubt you would flourish. I wish you could have
heard us cheering for you as you were recognized as
the best marksman in your battery. We always knew
you were an amazing shot, especially on the day you
shot all those blackbirds at the Roberts' house in
Canada using a crooked-shooting BB gun. I
remember Mr. Roberts saying you would not be able
to hit anything with that gun because it shot so
crooked. I also remember us all looking at him and
replying, "You don't know our boy! He is an amazing
shot!"

As a soldier in the United States Army, you have made us all proud already. We cannot wait to see where the Lord leads next.

As I read through the book of Psalms, I was reminded of another truth. You are not only a soldier in the US Army, but you are also a soldier in an even greater Army. You are a soldier of the Lord. The spiritual battlefield you face in His service is the most difficult battlefield you will ever experience. Follow your Commanding Officer. Fully submit to His lead. Do not let anything distract you. Shoot strait. Be fully committed.

> *2 Timothy 2:3-4 "Thou therefore endure hardness, as a good soldier of Jesus Christ. No man that warreth entangleth himself with the affairs of this life; that he may please him who hath chosen him to be a soldier."*

If you thought we cheered loudly and wildly for your marksmanship award and graduation, just wait to see how we cheer you on as you have spiritual victories! We are praying for you faithfully. You will always be our favorite Army guy.

With love,
Mom

> *3 John 1:4 "I have no greater joy than to hear that my children walk in truth."*

A Word from the Author

He was only four years old, and my son already had a fascination for the military. My husband and I overheard him one evening playing in the bathtub with his little green army men. We peaked around the corner to see what the pretend commotion was all about. Our little boy held an army soldier in each hand and acted out the most hilarious squabble imaginable.

"I wanna be da weader!" the first soldier cried. My son still struggled with sounding out his "L's," so this poor plastic army officer was reduced to being a weader instead of a leader.

Then the other army soldier responded, "No, I wanna be da weader!"

"You're always da weader! It's my turn to be da weader!" The argument continued for several minutes as my husband and I held back our giggles. Our imaginations had us roaring inside with laughter as we pictured how silly this would be if two real military men carried on this discussion.

If you ever wanted an interesting description of the book of Psalms, this is the picture. There is a battlefield in the heart of man. "I wanna be the leader!" he cries. He struggles surrendering to the leadership and authority of God. He wants to direct his own steps and plan his own life, all to his own injury.

The collection of songs in the book of Psalms, written under the inspiration of the Spirit by people who were well-versed in spiritual and physical warfare, gives a display of shock and awe, victories and defeats, and rebellions and surrenders in the battlefield of the heart.

As I journeyed through the book of Psalms in my personal quiet time, I found myself seeing the battlefield from a new perspective. Every day my own heart cried out, "I wanna be the leader!" yet I heard my Saviour call out through His Word, "Trust my lead."

My son is now grown and has become a real soldier in the military. He is learning daily to trust his commanding officer more and to submit to authority. He is learning the rewards as well as the repercussions of the decisions he makes regarding following the right leader. I, too, am learning to trust my Commanding Officer. I hear my heart cry out, "I wanna be the leader!" Simultaneously, I hear my Saviour call out, "Trust my lead."

Prepare your heart to be confronted, challenged, convicted, encouraged, and revealed daily in these Songs for the Battlefield.

Day 1
Stuck on Auto Play (Psalm 1:1-2)

Psalm 1:1 "Blessed is the man that walketh not in the counsel of the ungodly, nor standeth in the way of sinners, nor sitteth in the seat of the scornful."

Blessed: divinely favored, happy

There is no doubt we all have a desire to be divinely favored by the Lord. We all want to be happy. How do we get there? How do we live a blessed and happy life in the midst of battles?

For me, the last three days have been a battle. It has not been a physical battle, but a battle in my mind. For three days, I have had a song stuck in my mind. It is a song I heard many times when I was a teenager. It was played on the radio frequently. It is amazing that, twenty-five years later, this song I have not been listening to is suddenly ringing in my head, over and over. It is not a godly song at all, but it is stuck there, programmed in my memory, as if my brain was a computer. What happened?

When I was younger, I allowed ungodly counsel to enter my mind through my ears. Counsel can come in many different forms, but it enters through the eyes and ears. The things or people we listen to, watch, or read penetrate our hearts and minds. Those things, much like a computer, program our thinking. Our thinking then dictates our actions.

That is why it matters so much that we guard our eyes and ears. Through protecting those avenues we are guarding our hearts.

> Proverbs 4:23 "Keep thy heart with all diligence; for out of it are the issues of life."

When we listen to ungodly counsel, we begin a path of decline. We will begin to walk in that counsel. Before long we will feel comfortable with hanging around people and things that clearly do not please the Lord. Then we will relax amid wickedness.

Lot's life was a great example of this decline. Lot simply started walking in the direction of sinfulness (Sodom), at first hanging around the outskirts. (Genesis 13) Then he moved right in with the wickedness when he chose to move into Sodom to live. Toward the end, we see him sitting in the gates of the city in a position of leadership. (Genesis 19)

How do we keep our path from going down this same spiral? Guard what counsel goes into your ears and eyes. Begin inspecting each influence in your life, and ask, "Is this a godly counselor? Is this movie a help to my Christian growth, or a hindrance? Is this song going to help me walk in the Spirit today? Is this friend helping me grow more like Christ? Is this book programming my thinking in a godly fashion?"

What about situations like mine? The music (my ungodly counselor) was from years before when I was not protective of my heart. How do we deal with that? We must reprogram our computers, our minds.

Romans 12:2 "And be not conformed to
this world: but be ye transformed by the
renewing of your mind, that ye may
prove what is that good, and acceptable,
and perfect, will of God."

That renewing comes through faithfully putting good counsel in the mind. That good counsel comes from God's Word.

Psalm 1:2 "But his delight is in the law of
the LORD; and in his law doth he
meditate day and night."

If we want victory in our minds, and if we desire to keep our feet from that downward spiral in our spiritual walk, we need to have a:

1. **Delight in God's Word**- delight: treasure, satisfaction
2. **Deluge of God's Word**- deluge: overwhelm with a flood
   That deluge can be from a combination of reading God's Word, listening to preaching, spending time with godly influences, listening to godly music, etc.

What counselors are influencing you? Are you guarding your heart and thereby guarding your steps? Who are your counselors throughout your day and week?

Joshua 1:8 "This book of the law shall not
depart out of thy mouth; but thou shalt

meditate therein day and night, that
thou mayest observe to do according to
all that is written therein: for then thou
shalt make thy way prosperous, and then
thou shalt have good success."

When you follow this battle plan, you will be blessed, divinely favoured, and happy. Time for me to go listen to some godly music and meditate on Psalm 1:1-2.

Day 2
Plant Killer (Psalm 1:2-3)

I must openly confess that I am an expert plant killer. I do not mean to be. It is actually a natural talent I have. I have purchased plants thinking they would add beauty to my home, only to find them dead within a month. I have had people purchase them for me for gifts, and I mercilessly execute them as well. When we lived in the States, I finally resigned myself to artificial plants. One day as I was passing one of my fake green lilies in my house, my oldest child saw one of the leaves fall off the plastic plant and onto the floor.

"Mom, you are even killing the fake ones!" I am thankful he recognized my superior skills of plant killing. Nothing is impervious to my vicious talent. Yes, the government should have hired me to cure the kudzu problem.

If I were a plant of some sort, I would want to be one that was thriving, not a dead one and certainly not a fake one.

Psalm 1:2-3 "But his delight is in the law of the LORD; and in his law doth he meditate day and night. And he shall be like a tree planted by the rivers of water, that bringeth forth his fruit in his season; his leaf also shall not wither; and whatsoever he doeth shall prosper."

This tree described in Psalm 1 is thriving, green, and lush. It did not become that way by accident. The tree is not a wild tree. It was planted! Our Christian lives are no different. Pursuing growth and striving to walk in the Spirit daily are intentional actions, not accidental ones.

This planting also makes us stable. The location gives us a firm foundation because everything is conducive for us to have deep roots. God wants us to grow. He wants to plant us in specific places so that we will thrive and flourish with deep, strong, stable roots. What is the specific place He wants to plant us? According to this passage, He wants us planted in His Word and meditating on it day and night. That is how we become this tree. When we are planted in God's Word, our spiritual needs are supplied. We are planted by the rivers of water. Everything we need for our Christian growth is right there for us.

When we are well-established, we will become fruitful. A tree that produces is a valuable tree that blesses those around it. This tree only produces in his season, though. That tells me that patience is needed. This patient, but thriving, tree does not wither. It has endurance. Ultimately, this tree is successful in every one of his tasks. Everything the tree does prospers because he is planted in the right place, drinking from the right source.

Stable
Supplied
Fruitful
Patient

Enduring
Successful

All this because he delights in God's Word, and consistently stays in the Word.

> Deuteronomy 6:6-9 "And these words, which I command thee this day, shall be in thine heart: And thou shalt teach them diligently unto thy children, and shalt talk of them when thou sittest in thine house, and when thou walkest by the way, and when thou liest down, and when thou risest up. And thou shalt bind them for a sign upon thine hand, and they shall be as frontlets between thine eyes. And thou shalt write them upon the posts of thy house, and on thy gates."

> Joshua 1:8 "This book of the law shall not depart out of thy mouth; but thou shalt meditate therein day and night, that thou mayest observe to do according to all that is written therein: for then thou shalt make thy way prosperous, and then thou shalt have good success."

Get in the Word. Delight in the Word. Intentionally focus on God's Word throughout the day. Then you will be a tree even I cannot kill.

Day 3
Bulldozer Plans (Psalm 2)

Psalm 2:1 "Why do the heathen rage,
and the people imagine a vain thing?"

Being the mom of two boys with wild imaginations, I have a keen understanding of people imagining a "vain thing." Sometimes when things would happen, my boys would make bizarre and impossible statements. For example, if someone cut in front of us in line they would say, "We should have just rammed them with a battering ram!" Or if traffic was heavy they would say things like, "We need to just take a bulldozer and plow down through all this traffic!"

Really? A bulldozer? A battering ram? But such is the vain imagination of young boys. They imagined impossible things and treated them as realistic solutions. That is much like what the heathen and ungodly people of Psalm 2 are described as doing. They position themselves as if they are going to stand in God's way.

Psalm 2:2 "The kings of the earth set
themselves..."

They set themselves in a stance opposing God. Then they all gang up, and they think that there is safety in numbers.

> "...and the rulers take counsel together, against the LORD, and against his anointed, saying,"

What is their contention? Why are they angry? They think God and God's people are holding them back. They hate accountability and authority. They hate to be told "no."

> Psalm 2:3 *"Let us break their bands asunder, and cast away their cords from us."*

They make big plans of how to throw off His authority and His restraint. They make plans to take control. Just like when I would laugh at my sons' crazy bulldozer plans, God sits back and laughs at their impossible and silly ideas.

> Psalm 2:4 *"He that sitteth in the heavens shall laugh: the Lord shall have them in derision."*

God's rules and God's authority are not bonds or chains. His Word is safety. His laws are protection. His Word is a firm foundation.

Psalm 119:116 "Uphold me according unto thy word, that I may live: and let me not be ashamed of my hope."

Are we making bulldozer plans and going our own way? Are we refusing His authority in our lives? If so, we are acting like the heathen. Embrace His authority. Submit to His Word. It is not chains to bind us, but His Word is a shelter to protect us.

Day 4
Bandaging the Wounds (Psalm 3)

Can I be blunt? This morning I am tempted to fret about a situation someone is facing. I do not like to see people go through difficult things. I want to fix it. That is what the mom heart in me wants to do for people. I want to kiss the hurts and scraped knees, put cartoon character bandages on wounds, and give a candy bar to bring a smile.

This morning I sat down and read Psalm 3. God had the solution right there for me.

Psalm 3:3 "But thou, O LORD, art a shield for me; my glory, and the lifter up of mine head."

He is the solution to my worry. He is my hope. He is the lifter up of my head. So, what do I need to do?

Psalm 3:4 "I cried unto the LORD with my voice, and he heard me out of his holy hill. Selah."

I need to call out to Him with my worries. He will hear me.

Psalm 3:5 "I laid me down and slept; I
awaked; for the LORD sustained me."

He will give me peace, but I have to remember something important. I cannot play the role of Mrs. Fix-It. I cannot rush in, put my bandages on the wounds, and kiss it and make it all better. Mrs. Fix-It gets in the way of Mr. Healer-- Jesus.

Psalm 3:8 "Salvation belongeth unto the
LORD..."

Salvation belongs to Him. Not only is He the solution to my worry, but He is also the solution to the problems the people I love are facing. He is the answer, and He is better than a superhero bandage that covers up a wound. He heals the wound.

Day 5
Close Enemy (Psalm 3)

Who was he running from? In Psalm 3, was David running from the Philistines? The Syrians? The Amalekites? Who was he running from? Who was trying to kill him?

Take a deep breath. He was running from his own son, Absalom. Absalom had an army pursuing his father, David. Not only was David fleeing for his life, but he had the heartache of being the enemy of his own flesh and blood.

Sometimes our greatest heartaches come from those we least expect it. It would be easy to understand the world persecuting us or the lost causing trouble. It would be reasonable to expect wicked governments to seek our harm or for pagan tribes in the jungles to attack a missionary. What if the enemy is closer to home? What if the attack comes from family, friends, or church members?

David knew that kind of heartbreak. He knew that level of pain. He also knew where to turn.

Psalm 3:3 "But thou, O LORD, art a shield for me; my glory, and the lifter up of mine head."

David knew that when those closest to him seemed to forget they were family, God would never forget David belonged to Him.

Psalm 3:8 "... thy blessing is upon thy people. Selah."

God never forgets who His children are. When it seems that our greatest enemies are those who are supposed to be our greatest allies, turn to the "lifter up" of your head.

Proverbs 18:24 "... and there is a friend that sticketh closer than a brother."

Day 6
Belonging to Him (Psalm 4)

Compassion, hope, a declaration of how sweet life is with the Lord, a call to repentance, and a step-by-step instruction guide of turning to the Lord. That is Psalm 4 in a nutshell.

Psalm 4:1 "To the chief Musician on Neginoth, A Psalm of David. Hear me when I call, O God of my righteousness: thou hast enlarged me when I was in distress; have mercy upon me, and hear my prayer."

In the very first verse, David focused on who his God was. God helped him (enlarged him) before when he was in distress, so he knew that in his current situation he needed to call out to the Lord again.

When we face difficulties, we need to purposefully remind ourselves how God has taken care of us in the past. It builds our confidence that God will take care of us in the present and in the future.

Suddenly in the second verse, David turned his attention towards those who were against him.

Psalm 4:2 "O ye sons of men, how long
will ye turn my glory into shame? how
long will ye love vanity, and seek after
leasing? Selah."

These people were lying (leasing) and
gossiping about David. They were attacking his
character and reputation. What did David do? He
began explaining to them how good it was to belong
to the Lord, and that when they fought against God's
man, they were picking a fight against his God.

Psalm 4:3 "But know that the LORD hath
set apart him that is godly for himself:
the LORD will hear when I call unto him."

God separates his people for a special
purpose. He takes care of us because He has a
purpose for us. It is reasonable for us to be confident
that God will hear and answer our prayers because
we are His special treasure. David was not saying this
to boast. He was telling his critics how good God is
because he wanted them to repent and experience
this goodness.

Psalm 4:4 "Stand in awe, and sin not:
commune with your own heart upon your
bed, and be still. Selah."

Here is the call to repentance:

- "Stand in awe..." (literally to tremble.) Fear the Lord because He is holy.
- "... sin not..." (turn from your sins.)
- Commune with your heart. Meditate about the truth and the conviction God is giving you. He is drawing you.
- Be still and listen!

Psalm 4:5 "Offer the sacrifices of righteousness, and put your trust in the LORD."

- "Offer sacrifices of righteousness..." (the fruits of true repentance.)
- "... put your trust in the Lord..." (Call out to Him and believe on Him.)

Right here in Psalm 4 is the plan of salvation!

Psalm 4:6 "There be many that say, Who will shew us any good? LORD, lift thou up the light of thy countenance upon us."

Not only is the plan of salvation in Psalm 4, but also a call to share the good news. How shall they hear without a preacher? Who will show them any good?

Psalm 4:7 "Thou hast put gladness in my heart, more than in the time that their corn and their wine increased."

David shares again how good it is to belong to God. There is a joy in the heart regardless of circumstances. It is more abundant than the harvest at harvest time!

Psalm 4:8 "I will both lay me down in peace, and sleep: for thou, LORD, only makest me dwell in safety."

His salvation brings sweet peace and rest knowing God is in control, we belong to Him, and He takes care of His children.

If I could only convince you how sweet it is to be His! If you only knew the joy and peace it brings! I love being His child!

Day 7
My Way or the Highway (Psalm 5)

Have you ever heard that phrase "My way or the highway"? It basically means "We do it the way I choose or we part ways!" That is how wicked man thinks.

"I call the shots! I make my own way! What I say goes!" In Psalm 5, David declares a different story. We are completely dependent on God's grace.

Psalm 5:7-8 "But as for me, I will come into thy house in the multitude of thy mercy: and in thy fear will I worship toward thy holy temple. Lead me, O LORD, in thy righteousness because of mine enemies; make thy way straight before my face."

Thy mercy.
Thy fear.
Thy righteousness.
Thy way.

In pride man tries to make his own way. He tries to insert his demands and his words as truth and as authority. He wants to rely on self.

Psalm 5:9-10 "For there is no

faithfulness in their mouth; their
inward part is very wickedness; their
throat is an open sepulchre; they
flatter with their tongue. Destroy thou
them, O God; let them fall by their
own counsels; cast them out in the
multitude of their transgressions; for
they have rebelled against thee."

Their mouth.
Their inward part.
Their throat.
Their tongue.
Their own counsels.

All of that boils down to one thing in verse 10:
their transgressions.

David makes it clear that the difference
between the righteous and the wicked is one thing:
their trust in the Lord.

Psalm 5:11 "But let all those that put
their trust in thee rejoice: let them
ever shout for joy, because thou
defendest them: let them also that
love thy name be joyful in thee."

The wicked put their trust in self. The righteous
realize that the only hope we have is in God's mercy,
and therefore they put their trust in Him.

What are you depending on for salvation? Self or

God's mercy? What are you depending on for day-to-day living: self or God's way? What are you depending on in ministry: self or God's guidance? What are you depending on?

John 15:5 "I am the vine, ye are the branches: He that abideth in me, and I in him, the same bringeth forth much fruit: for without me ye can do nothing."

Day 8
Empty-Handed (Psalm 6)

My daughter has a sweet tenderness about her. When she was younger, if she did something wrong she would come to me with tears gushing out of her eyes. She would confess whatever it was she had done and ask me to forgive her. I was usually completely oblivious to her transgression. That did not matter to her. She knew she did wrong and did not want anything to interfere with our fellowship. She has always desired to please me. I imagine David being much like my daughter, though God is always aware of our transgressions.

Psalm 6:1 "O LORD, rebuke me not in thine anger, neither chasten me in thy hot displeasure."

David did not come to God presenting God with a list of reasons why he should not be punished or chastened. David knew he was guilty. He simply came seeking mercy from his God.

Psalm 6:2 "Have mercy upon me, O LORD; for I am weak: O LORD, heal me; for my bones are vexed."

My daughter never came up to me telling me how her good works should make up for her mistake. "Mom, you should not punish me because yesterday I cleaned my room without you asking me to."

David did not go to God and say, "You remember that giant I slayed?" No, he came empty-handed to the Lord knowing that he deserved discipline. He saw his sin for the vile act that it was. There was only one reason David gave in his plea.

Psalm 6:4 "Return, O LORD, deliver my soul: oh save me for thy mercies' sake."

God's mercy.

Do you try to justify your sin by balancing it with your good works? Do you come to God empty-handed when pleading for mercy? Do you plead for mercy, or is your sin no big deal in your eyes?

We need to see our sin as ugly as it really is. We also need to see our God as holy and as merciful as He really is.

Day 9
In My Defense (Psalm 7)

The enemy is vicious. He is a lion seeking to devour us. We are no match for him.

> Psalm 7:2 "Lest he tear my soul like a lion, rending it in pieces, while there is none to del*iver.*"

He is a liar, an accuser, and a slanderer. It is reasonable to assume that those in his service would do the same. The question is not what the enemy will do. He will do as he has always done. He comes to steal, kill, and destroy. His people will do his work. The question is: what will we do?

Will we panic? Will we be captivated by fear? Will we seek to defend ourselves? Or will we trust?

> Psalm 7:1 *"O LORD my God, in thee do I put my trust: save me from all them that persecute me, and deliver me:"*

Will we try to fight our battles or will we sit back in confidence that the Judge of all the earth will do right?

*Psalm 7:10 "My defence is of God,
which saveth the upright in heart."*

Do we welcome His inspection knowing the Lord searches and tries the heart? Would we welcome His Fatherly chastisement if we are indeed guilty? Are we willing to allow His Spirit to show us what we have sown, and are we willing to reap what we have sown?

*Psalm 7:3 "O LORD my God, if I have
done this; if there be iniquity in my
hands;"*

He is the Judge.

Psalm 7:8 "The LORD shall judge the people: judge me, O LORD, according to my righteousness, and according to mine integrity that is in me."

Our Defender.
Our Saviour.
Our God.
He is worthy of our trust.

Day 10
Small (Psalm 8)

I feel small.

When nighttime blankets the city and the sky is clear, I look up to see the glittering stars speckling the scene. I feel small and He seems big.

When my husband and I go for a hike and we climb the hills to look over the valley, we see the vast landscape. I feel small and He seems larger than ever in my eyes.

When we hop on a plane and fly for hours over the deep blue ocean, I look out the window of the plane through the cushion of clouds to gaze at the never-ending waters. I feel small and He grows exponentially in my heart and mind.

I feel so small.
Insignificant.
Unworthy of His thoughts or time.
And yet...

Psalm 8:4 "What is man, that thou art mindful of him? and the son of man, that thou visitest him?"

When I look at creation and see the sun, moon, and stars, I should feel small. I must feel small, and He should become an amazement and a wonder in my eyes. That is how it should be. It should also make it more precious that God, the Creator of all things, thinks on me and desires intimacy with me. Why would such a big God spend any effort or time on little me? He chooses to use the small things and the weak things to bring Him glory.

Psalm 8:2 "Out of the mouth of babes
and sucklings hast thou ordained
strength because of thine enemies,
that thou mightest still the enemy and
the avenger."

A mere babe and suckling am I! I am weak and small. But my Father, my Creator, my God is big!

Psalm 8:9 "O LORD our Lord, how
excellent is thy name in all the earth!"

Day 11
May I Take Your Order, Please? (Psalm 9)

Here is the restaurant scene: You walk in and sit at a table. Within minutes, a server walks up and takes your order. The server is ready and eager to meet your needs. Without delay, your drink is on the table, and not long after that your food arrives piping hot and ready to eat. All this was according to your requests. The server even returns periodically for drink refills and to clean away dirty plates.

Sometimes that is how we treat God. We walk in, sit down, expect Him to take our orders, and then we expect Him in timely fashion to fulfill our requests. Psalm 9 takes us into a different scene.

Psalm 9:1-2 "I will praise thee, O LORD, with my whole heart; I will shew forth all thy marvellous works. I will be glad and rejoice in thee: I will sing praise to thy name, O thou most High."

It ushers us into the throne room of the Most High God, the Judge of all the Earth.

Psalm 9:7 "But the LORD shall endure for ever: he hath prepared his *throne for judgment."*

Modern Christianity has become people-centered instead of Christ-focused. Our thoughts are consumed by "What can I get out of this?" instead of "What does my God deserve?"

The life we live, the church we attend, how we spend our time, our prayers, the music we listen to, the things we wear, and the people we hang out with are all decided by our perspective. Are we patrons sitting at a table waiting for God to serve us, or are we servants of the Lord kneeling whole-heartedly before His throne?

Let us follow Psalm 9 and come before His throne with praise, wonder, and humility. Let us sing of His marvelous works. Let us bow the knee, as well as the heart, as we come before Him with our requests, throwing ourselves at His feet for mercy. Celebrate His faithful and righteous judgments. Submit to His rightful authority. He is God, and we are not. Let us praise Him as He deserves.

Day 12
Thieves (Psalm 9:1-2)

I can feel it. I can hear the thieves whispering. Calling. I sense their caressing and gentle wooing. But...

Psalm 9:1 "I will praise thee, O LORD, with my whole heart..."

Thieves and robbers are they, yet they present themselves as sweet lovers. They have come to steal my love, my affection, my heart. But...

Psalm 9:1 "I will praise thee, O LORD, with my whole heart..."

Disguised, yet I see them now. Your Word removes their clever costumes.

- Entertainments
- Selfish pursuits.
- Relationships.

They strive to steal my heart. They seek to steal parts of my heart. If they succeed, my praise to my God will be shallow. Oh, but with my whole heart, Lord! You deserve my whole heart and my whole-hearted praise! When You have my whole heart, I cannot help but tell others about You!

Psalm 9:1-2 "I will praise thee, O LORD, with my whole heart; I will shew forth all thy marvellous works. I will be glad and rejoice in thee: I will sing praise to thy name, O thou most High."

With my whole heart...

Day 13
Running (Psalm 9:9-13)

Where do I run? When the oppression comes and the enemies are strong, where do I turn? Do I turn to people? The phone? Social media? Where do I go when the weight gets heavy and crushing?

Psalm 9:9 "The LORD also will be a refuge for the oppressed, a refuge in times of trouble. And they that know thy name will put their trust in thee: for thou, LORD, hast not forsaken them that seek thee."

Refuge: A place to go for safety, protection, comfort, security

It is a place to run. It is not a place that will come to me. I must choose to go to the refuge. It is a den, a cave, a fort. It is surrounded and safe, but I must choose to enter.

Often the place of refuge in the Bible is a cliff, a high place. In the high place, you are not enclosed, but you can see and identify the enemy clearly as he approaches. Defense is easy. Though not surrounded as in a cave or den, the high place refuge is secure. The open air allows us to see, to learn, and to grow while having the advantage of the upper ground. Sometimes our Refuge is a high place. He brings us up.

Psalm 9:13 "Have mercy upon me, O LORD; consider my trouble which I suffer of them that hate me, thou that liftest me up from the gates of death:"

In the high place He teaches me to spot the enemy. He teaches me how to defend, and I am safe.

He is my high place. He lifts me up. When I am low, will I run to Him? When the enemy puts great weights upon my chest, will I seek Him, or will I turn to other places that cannot give me safety and true relief?

He is my refuge.

Day 14
Post or Ponder (Psalm 9:16)

I am a teacher at heart. I love to share what I have learned. I love to help people in their walk with the Lord. Sometimes what God teaches me in the Bible is so exciting that I just burst at the seams waiting to share it with someone, but something He is teaching me is "haggaion selah."

Some words in the Bible are overlooked. They are ignored. Let me remind you that every word of God is pure. All scripture is profitable and is inspired by God, even the words haggaion selah.

Psalm 9:16 "The LORD is known by the judgment which he executeth: the wicked is snared in the work of his own hands. Higgaion. Selah."

Higgaion: a murmur, meditation.
Selah: a pause for thought.

It means to stop and think about it. It means to still your mind and focus on what was just said or done. These two words used together mean extra emphasis.

Sometimes I am so excited about what God is teaching me that I forget to stop. I forget to pause. I forget to still my mind and let His Word take full root in my heart. Sometimes He does not even mean for me to pass on what He is teaching me. Sometimes it is a lesson just for me alone at that time. Sometimes He wants me to ponder instead of post it on social media.

Luke 2:19 "But Mary kept all these things, and pondered them in her heart."

Look at Mary. She was a beautiful example. Jesus had just been born. He was placed in the manger, and suddenly a large group of shepherds came to visit and worship. Mary did not go running to post all about it on social media. She did not say much of anything. She kept the things in her heart and pondered. God had just done something amazing, and she chose to ponder instead of post. God was doing a great work in her heart, and she took time to higgaion selah so that it took full root in her heart and mind.

Colossians 3:16 "Let the word of Christ dwell in you richly in all wisdom; teaching and admonishing one another in psalms and hymns and spiritual songs, singing with grace in your hearts to the Lord."

Let the word of Christ dwell in you richly, higgaion selah. Then after it takes full root, after it springs forth with a renewed mind and a changed heart, teach! Read God's Word and higgaion selah! Watch God work and higgaion selah! Ponder more, post less, and watch God change you.

Day 15
Stop and Think (Psalm 9:16)

Think long and hard about it. You really need to take hold of these truths. Let them sink in, because your life-- your eternity-- depends on it.

> *Psalm 9:16 "The LORD is known by the judgment which he executeth: the wicked is snared in the work of his own hands. Higgaion. Selah."*

Higgaion. Selah.
Stop. Think. Meditate.

Here are the truths:
1. The Lord is Judge.
2. His judgments are right and just.
3. The wicked are bringing His judgment upon themselves. They are earning it!

This should make us ask a question, "Am I the 'wicked' it is talking about?"

It is easy to think, "I am not that bad. I am a good person." Maybe in man's eyes you are good, but what about in God's eyes? We love to exalt ourselves. We love to see ourselves higher than what we truly are, but here is what God's Word says about us:

*Romans 3:10 "As it is written, There
is none righteous, no, not one:"*

None of us are righteous. None of us are good.
We all come short.

*Romans 3:23 "For all have sinned,
and come short of the glory of God;"*

We are "the wicked." We are guilty, and we
must see ourselves as sinners before the Judge.

*Psalm 9:20 "Put them in fear, O
LORD: that the nations may know
themselves to be but men. Selah."*

The very first step in the plan of salvation is to
realize we are unrighteous man—sinners-- guilty
before the holy Judge. That is why we need the
Saviour.

Day 16
Taking the Reins (Psalm 10:4)

I expect it from the wicked, but what about when it happens with Christians? What about when I do it?

Psalm 10:4 "The wicked, through the pride of his countenance, will not seek after God: God is not in all his thoughts."

It is easy to understand when God does not cross the mind of the wicked. They are full of pride. They are determined to follow their own path. How often, though, do we as Christians do the same thing?

We wake up and God is not on our minds. We do not seek Him in His Word before we are off and running with the tasks of our day. When we skip devotions and prayer in the morning, are we not guilty of the same thing? Each time we face decisions in our lives, and we try to reason what we should do instead of stopping to pray, are we not guilty? When we do not seek God's Word for direction, are we not guilty?

The wicked operate their lives by their own rules and their own wisdom. God is not in their thoughts. Every time we take the reins of our lives and hearts, we are just as guilty.

How many decisions did I make today without thought to God and His Word? How many plans did I make on my own?

Choose today to be led by Him. Make Him the first thought of every day. Surrender your calendar, your clock, and your goals and dreams to Him.

Psalm 63:1 "O God, thou art my God;
early will I seek thee: my soul thirsteth
for thee, my flesh longeth for thee in a
dry and thirsty land, where no water is;"

Day 17
Mountain Retreat (Psalm 11)

I was a little afraid for myself, but I was petrified for my children. I remember when we were on deputation before moving to Asia, fear gripped my heart. Dangers we would face and sacrifices we would endure plagued my mind. I could deal with my own fears, but what I struggled with most was the fears I had for my children.

Poverty
Disease
Political instability
Lack of friends and family
Language barrier

The list of potential harmful obstacles was long and growing in my mind. We had people who asked us how we could take our children to such a dangerous place. When they asked those things, the fear grew in my heart. It all came to a peak one night in a church service. As the message was being preached, the Holy Messenger of Heaven pointed the Word directly to my heart. It was a piercing knife.

"Do you trust Me?" The question rang in the ears of my heart.

Psalm 11:1 "In the LORD put I my trust: how say ye to my soul, Flee as a bird to your mountain?"

My soul wanted to flee to the mountain, but His gentle voice kept calling out, "Do you trust Me?"

"Yes, Lord, I do, but..."

There was no room for "but..." as He continued to ask, "Do you trust Me?"

I looked back at all He had faithfully brought me through, and I remembered He could be trusted. I recalled the things the Bible declares Him to be, and my heart began to settle. I realized He loves my children even more than I do. Yes, He can be trusted. The path before us looked scary and the security of the mountain looked so comforting, but His arm wrapped around my heart. I realized that being in the caves of the mountain outside of God's will could never compare to being on the path walking with Him. Our children would follow us on the path, and He would be there with them, too.

We have now been in Asia for five years. Persecution of Christians has risen. There is a threat of a five-year jail term for anyone caught "proselytizing." The government would have no problem throwing children in jail, too. We have been asked, "So what are you going to do?"

The answer is simple. We will not retreat to the mountain. We will stay on the path with His arms wrapped around us. That does not mean that we will be immune to danger or harm. It does mean that He can be trusted no matter where His path takes us.

Yes, there are times when even my own soul cries out, "Run to the mountain!" but every time I sit down with His Word, I feel His arm around me. His Word steadies my steps on the path.

He can be trusted. He sits on the throne of Heaven and is in complete control.

Psalm 11:4 "The LORD is in his holy temple, the LORD'S throne is in heaven: his eyes behold, his eyelids try, the children of men."

The most exciting thing of all is that He never takes His eyes off our family even for a second.

Psalm 11:7 "For the righteous LORD loveth righteousness; his countenance doth behold the upright."

Day 18
Destroyed Foundations (Psalm 11)

It is a triangle, but it certainly is not what you would call a love triangle! There are three relationships in Psalm 11: The Lord and the righteous, the wicked and the righteous, and the Lord and the wicked.

The Lord and the Righteous
This Psalm shows how the Lord treasures the righteous. He watches over them and He tries them. He sends and allows difficulties in their lives for their growth and for His glory. During the trying, He never takes His eyes off His children.

Psalm 11:4 "... his eyes behold, his eyelids try, the children of men."
Psalm 11:5 "The LORD trieth the righteous..."
Psalm 11:7 "... his countenance doth behold the upright."

The righteous can trust Him during the trying, because God is in control and He loves righteousness.

Psalm 11:1 "In the LORD put I my trust..."
Psalm 11:4 "The LORD is in his holy

*temple, the LORD'S throne is in
heaven..."
Psalm 11:7 "For the righteous LORD
loveth righteousness..."*

The Lord and the Wicked

It is a stark contrast from God's relationship with the wicked. He does not send trials. He will rain down judgment.

*Psalm 11:5 "... but the wicked and
him that loveth violence his soul
hateth."
Psalm 11:6 "Upon the wicked he shall
rain snares, fire and brimstone, and
an horrible tempest: this shall be the
portion of their cup."*

The Righteous and the Wicked

The wicked aim their weapons at the righteous.

*Psalm 11:2 "For, lo, the wicked bend
their bow, they make ready their
arrow upon the string, that they may
privily shoot at the upright in heart."*

Why do they take aim at God's people? They hate God! They hate everything God's children represent because they hate what God represents. Do not be shocked when their bows are aimed at you.

2 Timothy 3:12 "Yea, and all that will live godly in Christ Jesus shall suffer persecution."

There is one verse of Psalm 11 I have not mentioned, and yet it is a pivotal question.

Psalm 11:3 "If the foundations be destroyed, what can the righteous do?"

The wicked throw off the very foundations of law, morality, and righteousness. What can the righteous do? Protest? Start a revolution? The answer to verse 3 is in verse 4.

Psalm 11:4 "The LORD is in his holy temple, the LORD'S throne is in heaven: his eyes behold, his eyelids try, the children of men."

When it seems the arrows of the wicked are aimed at the righteous and when it seems the very foundations of everything that is right, good, and holy are being destroyed, remember the One seated upon the throne of Heaven. He sees all. He is in control. He knows who belongs to Him.

What can the righteous do when the foundations begin to crumble? Turn to the One who never changes and is not intimidated by the devises of the wicked.

Day 19
Valuable, Yet Ceasing (Psalm 12:1)

Where are the godly and faithful men?

As Proverbs 31 declares the virtuous woman hard to find, Psalm 12 declares the godly, faithful man hard to find.

> *Psalm 12:1 "Help, LORD; for the godly man ceaseth; for the faithful fail from among the children of men."*

- Where are the men who will lead their homes to follow God?
- Where are the men who will teach their wives and their children God's Word?
- Where are the men who will stand for right even when it costs them greatly?
- Where are the men who are less talk and more action for the cause of Christ and the sake of the Gospel?
- Where are the men who will take their family to church faithfully?
- Where are the men who will stand by their word?
- Where are the men who will guard their eyes and their hearts?
- Where are the men who know their God?
- Where are the men who will turn off the television and say, "Sorry, but our family

is not watching that wickedness!"

They are ceasing. They are failing. If a virtuous woman is more valuable than rubies, what is the value of a godly, faithful man?

As a wife, I cannot declare "As for me and my house, we will serve the Lord." It is not my place. That is the husband's place. I am thankful for my husband who has declared our family will serve God. He is rare, valuable, and precious above all jewels.

As women, what can we do? Can we try to fix the men? Can we try to change them? No, our role is in the first two words.

Psalm 12:1 "Help, LORD..."

Pray! Pray for the men in our lives. Pray for men at church. Pray for the men in our family. Pray for our sons. Pray for our husbands. Pray for our fathers and brothers. Pray for our neighbors. Pray for our pastors and Sunday school teachers. Call out to God for Him to work in the lives of these men to make them godly and faithful.

Day 20
Double Heart (Psalm 12:2)

We have learned not to get too excited when the people here seem very friendly and go overboard trying to get closer to us.

Time after time, people have approached us with great flattering words about what good people we are and how they love Americans. They overindulge us with complements and even offer to go to church with us. (We certainly take them up on the church offer.)

Before long, the truth comes out. Their motives that were hidden finally come to the surface. They think they have slyly inserted their secret agenda, and yet the whole time they played the flattery game, we saw it coming.

"We are in need of money. Can you give us money?" Or, "My son is trying to get a visa to go to America. Can you get him a visa?"

When we assure them we neither have money to give them nor have the power to get a visa, the friendship is immediately finished. We never hear from them again. It breaks our hearts. We have a deep love for the people and a desire to show them true friendship. We long to help them in ways they do not understand, but often we are met with flattering lips and double hearts.

Psalm 12:2 "They speak vanity every one with his neighbour: with flattering lips and with a double heart do they speak."

If we understood how much God hates this form of vanity and deceit, we would never do it. God despises manipulation, flattery, and dishonest, secret motives. He desires us to be open, honest, and genuine with our neighbors, with our family, with our church, with our husbands, and certainly with Him.

We may fool ourselves in thinking we never do this, but we do. Every time we are nice to someone to get what we want we are guilty. Every time we paste on a smile in order to get our way we are guilty. Every time we play the part of the nice Christian to get God to do what we want we are guilty. We try to use our words to control and manipulate the situation. What happens when we do not get our way?

"Do it or I won't be your friend anymore!" I have heard young children make this declaration to their friends. As harsh as it is, at least they are open and honest about their motives and intents. As adults we use more subtilty, but we do the same thing to people and to God.

God is calling us to be honest and truthful. Manipulation is a wicked and deceitful practice. Flattery with hidden motives is a nasty soup of selfishness and lying. God is calling us to be genuine. People should be able to trust our motives are pure.

Day 21
His Perfect Word (Psalm 12:6)

God's Word. Powerful. Living. Inexhaustible. Amazing. Supernatural. Perfect.

Psalm 12:6 "The words of the LORD are pure words: as silver tried in a furnace of earth, purified seven times."

"The words of the LORD are pure words..."

His Word (all His words, even the little ones) are pure. They are perfect. They are not flawed in any way. They do not need changing. They do not need updating. They do not need correcting.

"... as silver tried in a furnace of earth..."

His Words withstand trials. They can take the heat without diminishing one bit. They can withstand the scrutiny of the harshest critic. They cannot be stopped or impeded. They do not need our help. They can stand on their own.

"... purified seven times."

God's Words will withstand the test of time. They are eternal. They cannot be destroyed. Throughout all time (past, present, and future) no matter who has hated them, who has attempted to destroy them, who has tried to silence them, God's Words will always be.

Luke 21:33 "Heaven and earth shall pass away: but my words shall not pass away."
Psalm 119:89 "For ever, O LORD, thy word is settled in heaven."

Now if we truly believe these powerful things about His Word, then why do not we read it faithfully every day? Why do not we live our lives by His Word? Why do not we compare everything with His Word to see if it is true? Why do we cower from those who oppose His Word? Why do we ignore parts of His Word that we do not like or that are harder to swallow? Why do we not memorize His Word and put it in our hearts? Why do we find the preaching of His Word boring? Why do we not share His Word more faithfully?

Day 22
Freedom of Speech (Psalm 12:4)

The Freedom of Speech in America is a gift, and I am thankful for it. It truly is one of our most treasured rights. The first amendment is a beautiful thing.

"Congress shall make no law respecting an establishment of religion, or prohibiting the free exercise thereof; or abridging the freedom of speech, or of the press; or the right of the people peaceably to assemble, and to petition the Government for a redress of grievances."

But what does the Bible say about the Freedom of Speech?

Psalm 12:4 "Who have said, With our tongue will we prevail; our lips are our own: who is lord over us?"

"You cannot tell me what I can and cannot say!" A wicked heart clings to the freedom of speech without recognizing there is a Higher Law that should regulate what we say. I am certainly thankful that our country recognizes the beauty of man being able to speak without government interference, but I am heartbroken when we do not recognize that the Lord should control the valve of our lips.

As an American, I may have freedom to say what I want, but as a Christian, I am called to lay that right at the foot of His throne.

Colossians 4:6 "Let your speech be alway with grace, seasoned with salt, that ye may know how ye ought to answer every man."
Ephesians 4:29 "Let no corrupt communication proceed out of your mouth, but that which is good to the use of edifying, that it may minister grace unto the hearers."
Proverbs 31:26 "She openeth her mouth with wisdom; and in her tongue is the law of kindness."

As a child of God, I do not have the right to speak lies, to gossip, to be immodest in my words and tone, to backbite, to slander, to use my words as weapons, to boast, to injure others, to speak out of turn, to speak without His permission, to exalt self, or to declare my opinion. God has declared His right of censorship.

Psalm 12:3 "The LORD shall cut off all flattering lips, and the tongue that speaketh proud things:"

When man attempts to take away our rights, we are quick to declare:

Acts 5:29 "... We ought to obey God rather than men."

What if man tries to give us rights that God chooses to regulate? I am thankful for the Freedom of Speech in America. I use it. I embrace it. God's Word is easily spread in America because of its existence. But my freedom is trumped by a Greater Law:

Acts 5:29 "... We ought to obey God rather than men."

How is your Freedom of Speech?

Day 23
Catching the Passion (Psalm 12:8)

People are watching. Someone always has eyes on us. As a mom, I have three pairs of eyes that have watched me. My children see what I do. They hear what I say. They see what I exalt in my life.

Just this past church service, I taught children's class. My youngest child is in the class. As I was teaching about how God had put an excitement and passion in my heart each morning for my morning devotions, I could tell he was listening closely. I talked about how every morning was just like Christmas and my Bible was the Christmas present. I could hardly wait each morning to see what God was going to give me.

A short time later, with great excitement and passion, my son walked up to me to show me his Bible. He had underlined a lot in it and jotted little notes in the margins.

"Mom! Look at Matthew 7! There is just so much in it! I read it and it was so good. It is packed with so much good stuff!"

I did not realize how contagious my passion for the Bible would be. I exalted God's Word, and in response, my son also exalted God's Word.

Psalm 12:8 "The wicked walk on

every side, when the vilest men are exalted."

We must be so careful what, or who, we exalt in our lives. People around us will catch a passion for what we exalt. They will imitate us as well as the person or thing we exalt. Why do the wicked surround us? Perhaps a lot of it is due to who we have exalted. We have idolized celebrities, athletes, musicians, movie characters, and political leaders who live ungodly lives. We praise them for their talents or their politics, but while praising them and exalting them, we have also inadvertently placed a stamp of approval on their actions, philosophies, speech, and lifestyles.

On the flip-side, how often do our children and the people around us see us exalting true heroes? How easily can they see our passion for God and His Word? Do names like Hudson Taylor and Adoniram Judson sound familiar to them? Would they know who Amy Carmichael was? Do we exalt the godly, modest women in our lives?

If we exalt wicked people, we help spread the infection of wickedness.

Day 24
Surrounded (Psalm 12:5)

I can walk just a few meters outside our gate and encounter dozens of idols and statues. I can look outside my bedroom window and see a shrine with a demon god made of stone. These idols do not see me. They have never heard my cries. They have never beheld my needs or my sadness. They have never beheld anything! They certainly will never arise to take action on my behalf.

But my God? Oh, He is different!

Psalm 12:5 "For the oppression of the poor, for the sighing of the needy, now will I arise, saith the LORD; I will set him in safety from him that puffeth at him."

- He sees. ("For the oppression of the poor...")
- He hears. ("... for the sighing of the needy...")
- He speaks. ("... now will I arise, saith the LORD...")
- In great compassion, He takes action. ("... I will arise... I will set him in safety from him that puffeth at him.")

Not only does my Father see, hear, and speak, but He also cares about my needs. He is not sitting by letting things pass. He is not hardhearted. He intervenes at the perfect time.

"... now will I arise..."

Did you catch that? "... now..." Now!

He waits for the perfect timing. It is not that He cannot see or hear. It is not that He does not care. He cares greatly about the needs of the poor, the needy, and the oppressed. Are we waiting on Him to do something? He knows when the "now" will come. While we wait for Him to arise and intervene, do not doubt His compassion or His ability. Do not be impatient and take over. Wait for the "now." Trust that He will arise and set you in safety in His perfect timing. Do not fret because of oppressors or circumstances. Your "now" will come and your Father will arise.

Day 25
Sight Problems, Not Circumstance Problems (Psalm 13)

When we are stuck in the waiting room and wonder if He remembers...

> *Psalm 13:1 "How long wilt thou forget me, O LORD? for ever?..."*

When it seems God is nowhere to be found...

> *Psalm 13:1 "... how long wilt thou hide thy face from me?"*

When it seems we wake up to the same pit every morning...

> *Psalm 13:2 "... having sorrow in my heart daily?..."*

It is a matter of sight, not a matter of circumstance.

Psalm 13:3 "... lighten mine eyes..."

When we are surrounded by darkness that seems to consume us, help us see the truth, Lord! Fill our vision with the light of Your Word. Our circumstances may not change, but help us give You glory so that our enemies will be speechless.

Psalm 13:4 "Lest mine enemy say..."

You have proven yourself merciful in the past, and we have trusted Your love for us.

Psalm 13:5 "But I have trusted in thy mercy..."

Who You are has given us great confidence for the future. It has built our faith for current and future things.

Psalm 13: 5 "...my heart shall rejoice in thy salvation."

The more we remember Your faithfulness and Your undying love for us, the more the darkness fades away and a song rises in our hearts.

Psalm 13:6 "I will sing unto the

*LORD, because he hath dealt
bountifully with me."*

When we are surrounded and overtaken by
dark circumstances, focus on truth. God is good, and
He loves us. Focus on His character and how good
He has been in the past. He is the same God today
as He has always been. Our circumstances have not
changed God or His love for us. Sing praises for His
goodness, and those genuine praises of trust will
wash away the darkness in spite of the circumstances
we face.

Day 26
The Mystery (Psalm14:1)

I love a good mystery. I love trying to piece together the clues that are given in the story line and trying to figure out who did the crime. I love it when the storyteller gives all the clues but does not reveal the perpetrator until the end.

But the Bible is a different kind of mystery. From the very beginning it tells us "Who dunnit."

Genesis 1:1 "In the beginning God created the heaven and the earth."

Throughout the Bible it tells us all the clues of the mystery, too. Not only do we read about the clues, but we also get to see, examine, and experience the clues.

I look out over creation and know "Who dunnit." I see the intricacies of the human body. I see the perfection of the human eye. I see the majesty of the huge mountains, and I see the details of a tiny leaf that makes food for the tree. I breath in oxygen and breath out carbon dioxide. That same leaf takes in carbon dioxide and gives me oxygen. I know "Who dunnit."

I gaze at the stars and study the orbits of the planets. I sit in the warmth of the sun, and I enjoy the sound of the rain on the roof. Oh, I know "Who dunnit."

I have witnessed the birth of a baby. I have watched him take his first breath. I have experienced love. I know "Who dunnit."

My very own conscience declares there is a God, and my heart desires to worship. I sense right and wrong and know that I will answer to Someone for it. Those things were placed in my heart. I know exactly "Who dunnit."

Then I read God's Word and my suspicions are confirmed. He is the culprit who made all of creation. He is the one who gave man a desire to worship. He is the one who has written His law on our hearts so that we know there is a God to whom we will answer. He even declares, "I did it!" The Bible is His written confession.

Surrounded by the clues, his confession in our hands, and there are still people who want to accuse someone else of doing these things.

Psalm 14:1 "The fool hath said in his heart, There is no God..."

Day 27
Deodorant (Psalm 14:3)

"Why do bad things happen to good people?"

We have been asked this question more times than I can count. The problem is that the question itself is faulty. Where are these good people? In man's eyes we might see good people, but from the perspective of a holy God it is a much different picture. What does He see?

> Psalm 14:3 "They are all gone aside, they are all together become filthy: there is none that doeth good, no, not one."

Why is there such a contrast in view? Why do we see good people when God paints such a tainted picture of man?

I live in a culture that does not use deodorant. Deodorant is rarely available here, and it has only been spotted on a shelf a couple of times in recent years here. Our family uses deodorant, but we bring it with us from the States to insure we have it.

Sometimes we attend special church services or conferences in the heat of the summer. During these services, the room is typically packed with people sitting shoulder-to-shoulder. There is no air conditioning, so it gets extremely hot. People are sweating. Since they do not use deodorant, the aroma in the room becomes almost tangible to those of us who wear deodorant. Our noses are accustomed to clean, pretty smells. The people here are not affected by the smell. Their sense of smell for body odor has been dulled by their habits.

It is the same with the Lord. He is holy, clean, and pure. His sense of smell is keen and fully aware of the stench of sin. While we look around us and are unaffected by the horrid aroma of sin, He breathes in and cringes. The only time we are impacted is when someone seems to stink more than usual. The problem is that we do not smell our own stench.

We must understand that God does not owe any of us anything. We all stink with the putrid smell of our sin. Yet, God came down and dwelt among us. Surrounded by our stench, He remained perfect and pure. He endured our lives' odors so that He could rescue us. Nailed on a cross shoulder-to-shoulder with those drenched in the stench of sin, surrounded by the filthy smell, He endured it all for our sake.

Why do bad things happen to good people? There was only one good Person who ever lived on earth. His name is Jesus.

Day 28
Abiding and Dwelling (Psalm 15:1)

God desires it greatly and has desired it since the beginning. The question is: do we?

Psalm 15:1 "LORD, who shall abide in thy tabernacle? who shall dwell in thy holy hill?"

Oh, how quickly we often skim through His Word without stopping to think about its depths! This one verse drips with the heart of God as well as the desire of a man who loved God.

Abide- to sojourn, to turn aside from the road traveled and stay

Dwell- to inhabit, to rest

Tabernacle- a temporary place, representing the presence of God, traveled with the people

The holy hill- Mt. Zion, where the Temple was built, a permanent place

What does God desire? He longs for sweet, constant, consistent communion with man. In this verse, David asks, "Lord, who is the person that dwells in Your presence consistently? Who resides in sweet communion and fellowship with You? With whom do You go throughout their day as the tabernacle traveled with the children of Israel? Who comes to You and resides with You in fellowship as if they lived in the temple itself?"

As I read ths Psalm, I think of Enoch.

Genesis 5:24 "And Enoch walked with God: and he was not; for God took him."

Enoch walked with God. This was not talking about him strolling down the road with God as you and I would stroll with a friend. It was talking about him abiding in a constant state of close communion and intimacy with God. Oh, to have that level of closeness!

I think of the time when Jesus spoke of abiding and the results of abiding in Him and He in me.

John 15:5 "I am the vine, ye are the branches: He that abideth in me, and I in him, the same bringeth forth much fruit: for without me ye can do nothing."

I have a deep desire and longing to be fruitful for His glory, but it will never happen until I learn to abide, to dwell, and to walk with God. I desire a powerful and effective prayer life, but Jesus said:

John 15:7 "If ye abide in me, and my

*words abide in you, ye shall ask what
ye will, and it shall be done unto you."*

The key is abiding, dwelling, and walking with God.

- Do I hunger for it?
- Do I crave it?
- Do I settle for less throughout my day?
- When I close my Bible after morning devotions, does the intimate fellowship stop?
- Who is this person that abides in His tabernacle and dwells in His holy hill? How can it be me?

He longs for that fellowship. Do I?

Day 29
Walk, Work, Words (Psalm 15:2)

Sweet, close, intimate communion.
We want it, but are we willing to be what it takes, and do what it takes, to have it? Who is this man who has this level of fellowship with the Lord?

Psalm 15:2 "He that walketh uprightly, and worketh righteousness, and speaketh the truth in his heart."

His walk, work, and words are consumed by righteousness and truth.

His Walk
His daily life is a fruit of his righteous thinking. His testimony is pure. He has standards of purity, and holiness matters to him. He does not look like the world, think like the world, or act like the world. He has crawled up on the altar and presented himself as a living sacrifice, fully submitted and committed.

Romans 12:1-2 "I beseech you therefore, brethren, by the mercies of God, that ye present your bodies a living sacrifice, holy, acceptable unto God, which is your reasonable service. And be not conformed to this world: but be ye transformed by the renewing of your

mind, that ye may prove what is that
good, and acceptable, and perfect, will of
God."

His Work

Everything he does is decided by
righteousness. He is not content to warm a pew. Just
as he has placed himself on the altar, his time,
energy, efforts, and resources have also been placed
on the altar. He seeks the things of God.

*Matthew 6:33 "But seek ye first the
kingdom of God, and his
righteousness; and all these things
shall be added unto you."*

His Words

Truth matters to him. It is not just what he says.
It is in his heart.

"... speaketh the truth in his heart."

He loves God's Word. He treasures it. He
delights in it. He not only operates his life by it, he
tempers his thoughts by it. Truth governs his love,
desires, and passions.

*Psalm 1:2 "But his delight is in the
law of the LORD; and in his law doth
he meditate day and night."*

When our life, our labor, and our love are consumed by righteousness and truth, we will walk with our righteous God in tender communion and fellowship.

Amos 3:3 "Can two walk together, except they be agreed?"

Day 30
Loyal (Psalm15:3)

Loyalty runs deep in my family. My Dad was one of the most loyal people I have ever known. If you treated his family with disrespect, it was as if you treated him with disrespect. He and his family were a package deal. If you loved him, you had to love his family.

My Dad passed that deep rooted sense of loyalty to me. That same loyalty has now been passed on to my oldest son.

God's loyalty is deeper than ours. His loyalty is rooted in an unselfish love. He declares that if we love Him, we will also love the things He loves. He loves people.

The two greatest commands were given, and for me to walk intimately with God and abide in Him both commands matter.

Mark 12:30-31 "And thou shalt love the Lord thy God with all thy heart, and with all thy soul, and with all thy mind, and with all thy strength: this is the first commandment. And the second is like, namely this, Thou shalt love thy neighbour as thyself. There is none other commandment greater than these."

It matters to God how I treat others because He loves people. If I cannot treat others right, my fellowship with Him will be impacted.

Psalm 15:3 "He that backbiteth not with his tongue, nor doeth evil to his neighbour, nor taketh up a reproach against his neighbour."

A person who walks intimately with God will have control over his tongue. He will not gossip about his neighbor. He will not do things that will harm his neighbor or injure his neighbor's testimony. He will not slander his neighbor, and he also will not listen to those who speak ill of his neighbor. Why? Because this man knows God loves his neighbor, and it is a package deal. To truly love God, we must also love what God loves.

Day 31
Admiring Heroes (Psalm 15:4)

Who are your heroes?
Who do you want to be like?
Who do you quote on social media?
Who do you praise?
Who do you admire?
Who do you respect?

I remember watching the Super Bowl a couple of years ago with some friends. It was a great game to watch. I remember several times saying I liked one of the quarterbacks because he was a great guy. I called him a "classy player" and exalted his character as a good sportsman.

When his team won, a reporter dashed over to his side to interview him. He was asked what his plans were for the rest of that evening. He declared, "I'm gonna drink a lot of beer tonight... Budweiser."

My heart was deflated. Yes, I was sad that he would choose to spend his time that way, but I was even more heartbroken that I had exalted this man in any fashion in front of others, including children. With my words and admiration, I had just given my stamp of approval on this man because of his abilities and his on-the-field conduct without consideration of what he was truly like as a person.

Psalm 15:4 "In whose eyes a vile person is contemned; but he

honoureth them that fear the
LORD..."

If we desire to be that person who walks with God and communes with Him intimately, we have to be careful what or who we exalt and admire. They may handle a sports ball well, but what are they like off the field? They may have some great political policies, but what is their character? They may star in some fun and exciting movies, but what are they like when the cameras are off and the makeup and costumes are removed?

Can you imagine walking with a friend in fellowship and then telling that friend how much you admire someone who had deeply offended your friend? It would not make good conversation. Sin is a stench in our Friend's nostrils.

Can you imagine walking with a friend and talking with them about someone who had given everything (even their lives) for your friend? Oh, there would be lots to talk about! Can you imagine the fellowship as you commune with your Friend about missionaries, past and present, who loved your Friend so much that they left their homes behind to tell others about Him? What about a conversation on a pastor and his wife who were faithful even among persecution and ridicule?

The people we honor shows what is in our hearts. When we honor the people God honors, it shows that our hearts are in tune with His. It shows that we treasure the things He treasures. It is no wonder that a man who contemns (despises) vile persons and honors those that fear God have such close fellowship with Him!

So, who do you admire?

Day 32
I Promise (Psalm 15:4)

There are certain people in my life that I know when they give their word that they will do something, you can count on it. They promise to do something, and they take their commitments seriously. You do not have to remind them several times. You do not have to ask them if they have forgotten about it. It will be done because they have made a commitment. Even when that commitment turns out to be harmful to them (financial loss, property loss, time loss, causes extreme difficulty) they will not try to back out of that commitment.

> *Psalm 15:4 "... He that sweareth to his own hurt, and changeth not."*

That is the kind of people that walk intimately with God, because that is how God is. He keeps His promises. When He makes a commitment, even one that costs Him greatly, He will not back out of that commitment.

Way back in Genesis 3:15, He promised to send a Saviour. He kept His promise even though it cost Him greatly. He sent His Son to die on the cross for us. He promised to send the Comforter, and He did. He promised to return, and we can count on Him keeping that promise, too.

God expects us to be people of integrity who keep our promises and commitments. We should not back out of those commitments when we realize they will cost us something.

Day 33
Money Matters (Psalm 15:5)

"What's in it for me?"

That is the tragic mindset of people in America today, even professing Christians. That thinking governs our decision making. It dictates how we do things. It even controls what church we choose to attend. We want to know what programs there are and how they plan on entertaining our children. We are always looking for a benefit or advantage.

That is not the thinking controlling those who walk intimately with God. They are not looking for gain or advantage. They cannot be manipulated by the allurements of prosperity.

Psalm 15:5 "He that putteth not out
his money to usury, nor taketh reward
against the innocent..."

It was a common practice during the time of David for people with money to loan money to people in desperate need and then charge an extreme interest rate. They took advantage of people in need in order to get more money.

If we want to be someone who fellowships intimately with the Lord, we cannot be focused on selfish gain, especially at the expense of those in need. Life is not about accumulating wealth. It is not about the American dream. It is about loving God and loving others. We certainly cannot love others if we see their tragedy as an opportunity for advantage.

Taking reward against the innocent: dishonesty for selfish gain

Another common practice in David's time was the taking of bribes. If someone wanted to get his neighbor in trouble, he would approach a third party and bribe them to be a witness before the authorities against the innocent neighbor.

Exodus 20:16 "Thou shalt not bear
false witness against thy neighbour."

Financial gain or advantage was motivation for dishonesty. It seems foreign to us, but let me put it in a modern context.

You have a stack of expired coupons. You know that if the cashier does not check the dates, the computer will scan them anyway. You go ahead and attempt to use them knowing that it is dishonest. The cashier scans the coupons through and does not check. You walk out saving $8 in expired coupons and tell yourself that if the computer lets it slide through then it is not your problem. That is dishonesty for financial gain. Satan just bribed you with $8. You may not have been a false witness against a neighbor, but you defrauded your neighbor for financial gain.

When we take advantage of people or when we are dishonest with people for personal gain, we cut off that close fellowship with God. He is honest, compassionate, and truthful. He wants us to be the same way. He also wants us to realize He is our provider. We do not have to manipulate or work the system to have our needs met. He does not want us focused on personal gain. He wants us focused on following Him.

This is how God wants us to think of personal gain of any sort, whether honest or dishonest, whether honorable or selfish:

> Philippians 3:7-8 "But what things were gain to me, those I counted loss for Christ. Yea doubtless, and I count all things but loss for the excellency of the knowledge of Christ Jesus my Lord: for whom I have suffered the loss of all things, and do count them but dung, that I may win Christ,"

Yes, following the will of God costs us things, but God provides us with gain greater than any treasures this world has to offer. He is our provider and will take good care of us.

Day 34
Quake Proof (Psalm 15:5)

If you have never experienced a major earthquake, I pray you never do. The most uncomfortable feeling of an earthquake is that the ground beneath you that had always been sturdy and unmovable is shaking and knocking you off your feet. When we walk on the ground, we walk with confidence because it is stable, but when an earthquake hits, suddenly the confidence is shattered. The ground that is supposed to be still begins to violently twist, shake, and turn.

We are all searching for stability in life. We all crave to be planted on a firm foundation. God's Word teaches us how to go from spiritual earthquakes to ground which will never move, ground we can stand on with confidence that will never be shaken.

Psalm 15:5 "... He that doeth these things shall never be moved."

I love the word "never" in this verse. If I could prevent an earthquake, I certainly would do it! What if I could prevent a spiritual quake?

The person who does the things in Psalm 15 is planted on a firm foundation and is unmovable. That person who treasures righteousness, adores God's Word, has temperance, loves people, and pursues

God is stable.

How do we become that person? How do we consistently walk closely with the Lord-- so close that we cannot be shaken?

We can only do it by God's enabling. We can only do it as we abide in Him and learn to let Him shape us and change us. He wants us to walk with Him. He craves our fellowship. He wants us planted on a firm foundation, stable and unmovable, but do we want it enough to forsake our own way? Do we crave it enough to give up our own path and our own will?

Day 35
Eggs and Rice (Psalm 16:2)

I see it all the time-- almost every day. People lay food offerings in front of statues. They drape flowers on cars and bow down to their own vehicles. They set small bowls of rice, eggs, fruits, and sometimes money in front of trees and rocks, statues and cars, pictures and animals. One day a year they bow down to their own dogs and feed them special foods. The people feel they are doing some special service to these gods, these gods that cannot help themselves. But the God of Heaven? The Creator of all things? The only true God?

Psalm 16:2 "O my soul, thou hast said unto the LORD, Thou art my Lord: my goodness extendeth not to thee;"

Our goodness does not "extend" to God because He is not dependent on us. He needs nothing! He does not need my help. He does not need me to feed Him or clothe Him. He is not dependent on me in any fashion.

Before you are quick to think how foolish people are who worship these helpless idols, stop and think about how we sometimes treat God. When we attend church as if it is our duty so that God will be happy, we have just treated Him like an idol. Instead of a bowl of rice and eggs, Church becomes the little offering we set before Him. When we act like church is our sacrifice and we are doing our part by sitting on a pew, we have treated Him like an idol. When we throw money in the offering plate and feel we have sacrificed greatly, we have treated Him like an idol.

God does not need us. He does not need our money. He is not impressed by our dutiful church attendance or our financial obligations placed in the offering plate.

So why do we attend church? Why do we give? It is commanded, yes, but there is more to it than that. We obey His command because we trust Him. We trust that gathering with other believers in fellowship and worship is good for us and will help us grow. He is worthy of our worship and adoration, because the God who needs nothing from us loves us. It is about a relationship. You cannot have a relationship with a statue. Our God desires to fellowship with us. Does He need our worship? No. If He wanted He could make the stones cry out in worship and praise. In His love for us, though, He has opened that opportunity to us.

Why give? Again, yes, it is commanded, but it is an act of trust and love. We give, not because we want to earn His favor as idol worshipers giving to a statue, but we give because we have a love for the things He loves. We give because we have surrendered our hearts and lives (and all our possessions) to Him. It is all about relationship, and that is something that those who worship idols cannot experience.

How is your church attendance? Is it sporadic because it is a sacrifice? Is it consistent but obligatory? Has church become your offering in a little bowl, or is it about a relationship with your Father? What about your giving? Does it make you feel good about yourself when you give? Do you feel you are sacrificing or doing your part to help God out, or have you surrendered everything you have to Him because you trust Him? When you give, is it with a joyful, cheerful heart because you love the things He loves and want to be a part of it?

Are you bringing Him a bowl of rice and eggs, or are you bringing Him your heart?

Day 36
Saintly Delight (Psalm 16:2-3)

There is a problem in our churches today. When we were on furlough we spotted it more often than we imagined. It was shocking! We would enter a church and would notice the people seemed very distant from us. We understood. We were visitors and some people did not know us. The shocking part was that we noticed they were distant from each other too.

When they would enter the church, the people would head straight to the pew, sit through service, give quick glances and smiles, and then beeline out the door when the service was finished. Literally five to ten minutes after service was finished the church was again empty. No fellowship. No hugs and laughter. No communion between church members. Certainly no getting to know the visiting missionary! At one church, even the pastor did it. On his way out the door the pastor asked my husband to make sure the doors were locked when he left.

Psalm 16:2-3 "... my goodness
extendeth not to thee; But to the
saints that are in the earth, and to the
excellent, in whom is all my delight."

In David's Psalm, we see a different picture. His goodness was focused where the need was. He loved the saints. He delighted in them. They were his treasure and he was concerned about their needs.

There was joy and compassion.

Here is something else interesting: this is considered a Messianic Psalm. (Wording in verse 10 gives a clue to that.) What is a Messianic Psalm? Imagine Jesus, the Messiah, saying these things. His goodness is turned toward those in whom He delights. He loves the saints. He loves the church. He died for the church. He desires close communion and tender fellowship with the church. He fellowships with and serves the saints. His goodness is extended toward them.

How do you feel about your fellow church members? Do you delight in them? Do you enjoy spending time with them? Is your goodness extended toward them? Do you make a point to get to know them, serve them, and love on them? When is the last time you intentionally made time to fellowship with different members of your church family? Do you regularly visit them or invite them to your home? Do you enjoy spending time with them before, during, and after church service, or do you make a beeline for the door because your delight is in whatever is for lunch? Where is your goodness focused?

John 13:35 "By this shall all men know that ye are my disciples, if ye have love one to another."

Day 37
Enough (Psalm 16:5)

My kids, especially the oldest boy, used to ask me a question. As we drove around in our purple minivan accomplishing our tasks of running errands and grocery shopping, they would ask, "If you could have any car in the world, what would you have?"

My answer never satisfied them and always perplexed them. "This one."

"Mom!" Frustrated sighs would echo through the van. "No, really. Any car in the world, what would it be?"

"This one. Really." My children could not understand my contentment with our minivan. They expected me to proclaim my love and adoration for a Mustang GT 500 (whatever all that means) or a Ferrari. Anything but a plain old minivan.

"Why this one?" they would finally ask.

"It is paid for. It meets all our needs. It runs faithfully and does not let us down," I would always answer. I did not bother also explaining that our minivan held tons of precious family memories and adventures. Young kids are not into mushy stuff like that.

They did not understand my answer back then, but as they are getting older they are beginning to comprehend.

*Psalm 16:5 "The LORD is the portion
of mine inheritance and of my cup:
thou maintainest my lot."*

Did you know the Levites did not receive a land inheritance like the rest of the children of Israel? As the other tribes were receiving their land portion, God declared Himself as the Levites' inheritance. The Levites were the priests and they had a special task. Their job was a great honor. Tthat would be their portion, but was God enough for them? Is God enough for us?

I think back on our minivan. It was perfect for our family. It met our needs. We all fit in it comfortably. We could easily load groceries and luggage and sports equipment. We could tote friends back and forth with us to places. We could sleep in it like a tent if we decided to go on a quick, impromptu camping trip and have an adventure. It was great for long trips. Like I said, it was perfect. It did not have the glitz and glamour of a Ferrari, but a Ferrari certainly would not have been practical. It would have robbed us of all our adventures, memories, comfort, and ease.

God is perfect for us. He meets our every need. The shiny trinkets of this world cannot do that. The devil tries to hold those sparkling treasures in front of us to tempt us, and yet God says, "I am enough."

Our minivan was paid for. One of the happiest days was when we made our last payment on our van. It certainly freed up finances, time, and energy. Our relationship with the Father is paid for by the blood of His Son. I do not have to work for it. The trinkets of this world, though, have a heavy price to pay, often a lifetime of burden and obligation. No thank you. God is enough.

Our purple minivan, affectionately named Purpy, was a faithful vehicle. She rarely had any problems. We knew her well. She was reliable. We took her all over the eastern side of the States and even up into Canada. We were not afraid of her leaving us stranded. She was dependable. And God? He is more dependable than some old minivan! He never lets us down. He never neglects or forgets us. He supplies every need.

God is enough.
When friends forget you... God is enough.
When the world despises you... God is enough.
When you feel alone... God is enough.
When you are overwhelmed... God is enough.
When stress wants to grip your heart... God is enough.
When you do not know what to do... God is enough.
When your heart is breaking... God is enough.

Do not set your affections on the things of this world. They will never satisfy. They will never meet your needs. They will never bring joy. Be content with the Lord. He is the portion of our inheritance, and He is enough.

Psalm 16:5 "The LORD is the portion

of mine inheritance and of my cup:
thou maintainest my lot."

Day 38
Yarn Treasures (Psalm 16)

For several years, our family did something fun and unique at Christmas. My husband and I hid the children's Christmas gifts around the house. We attached yarn to the gifts and ran the yarn all through the house in crazy places. The yarn was color-coded so that one child had to follow the red yarn to find her gifts, one had to follow blue yarn to find his gifts, and the last child had to follow the green yarn to find his gifts. When the children got up the next morning, we handed them the end of their yarn and watched as they followed the webbed maze of yarn to their treasures. As long as they followed the yarn, they always found each treasure. The yarn was their treasure map and guide.

Psalm 16 is a treasure map. What treasures will it lead us to find?

Gladness and Hope

Psalm 16:9 "Therefore my heart is glad, and my glory rejoiceth: my flesh also shall rest in hope."

Life, Fullness of Joy, and Pleasures

Psalm 16:11 "Thou wilt shew me the path of life: in thy presence is fullness

*of joy; at thy right hand there are
pleasures for evermore."*

As long as we follow our treasure map, we will find the treasures. Where does this map take us?

When my children were following their yarn maps, it often became a complicated web. There were twists and turns. There were times the yarn overlapped. There were times the yarn went in bizarre places (like when one child had to go outside in the deep snow, through the minivan, and then back inside the house, all while still in his pajamas!) No matter how complicated the path, as long as the child stayed with the yarn, he or she found the treasures.

Each child also had his own path. No two paths were the same, but there were some things they all had in common. They had to follow their own paths. They had to stay on their own paths faithfully. Mom and Dad laid out all their paths. Each child had to follow yarn. (We did not have yarn for one child and a chain for another.)

In life, each of us has unique paths. Mine will not look like yours. Our paths can get complicated, but if we stay on track, we will have these treasures. There are some things about our paths that are the same. Our paths have been laid out by our Father.

What is the "yarn" of Psalm 16? What path must we follow? Here is the path to the treasures:

Contentment (vs5)
Knowing God is enough (He is the portion of our inheritance.)

Thankfulness (vs6)
Knowing we are blessed with a goodly heritage.

Praise (vs7)
Blessing the Lord because He is worthy.

Obedience (vs7)
Following His Word (Counsel and instruction)

Christ-centered Foundation (vs8)
Keeping Jesus the priority in our lives.

An Eternal Focus (vs10)
We serve a risen Saviour, and because of that we will also rise!

Abiding in His Presence (vs11)
In His presence is fullness of joy!

As my children were following their yarn, they only got one present at a time, but as we follow the path God lays out for us we can have each of our treasures every day. The key is to stay on the path.

Contentment, Thankfulness, Praise, Obedience, Christ-centered Foundation, Eternal Focus, and Abiding in His Presence

Are you lacking peace, hope, joy, and gladness? Get back on the path.

Psalm 16:11 "Thou wilt shew me the path of life: in thy presence is fulness

*of joy; at thy right hand there are
pleasures for evermore."*

Day 39
Pants on Fire (Psalm 17:1)

"Liar, liar, pants on fire!"

It be interesting if that really would happen-- if someone lied, and then you always knew it because their pants burst into flames. It would certainly make interesting political speeches. Unfortunately, it would probably happen to all of us in the middle of prayer.

Feigned: adj. False, fraudulent, deceitful, pretend

Have you ever had feigned lips in prayer?

> *Psalm 17:1 "A Prayer of David. Hear the right, O LORD, attend unto my cry, give ear unto my prayer, that goeth not out of feigned lips."*

This was not just a song. It was a prayer. David was in a crisis. He was likely on the run from Saul at the time. (Times of crisis are a persuasive motivator for an improved prayer life.) David called out to God and declared his prayer was not from false, deceitful, or pretend lips.

So how exactly does one pray with feigned lips?

Absent-minded, Thoughtless Prayer

Have you ever started praying, "Lord, thank you for this day. Thank you for this food..." only to realize you were not about to eat? You were not even sitting at the dinner table! You just said that phrase out of habit. You were praying thoughtlessly.

Prayer is communion with our God. It is supplication, praise, intercession, thanksgiving, and a form of worship. When we pray without thinking about what we are saying, it is feigned lips. It is pretend. We are not really communing with God. We are just speaking empty words.

Apathetic Prayer

Have you ever prayed about something, but you really did not care about the answer to that prayer? You were just praying because it was a prayer request on your prayer list. In your mind you checked it off your list so that you could tell the person, "I prayed for you." It made you feel spiritual and made you look good in front of others, but did you really care about their prayer need? If we were honest, we would often have to say, "I prayed for your need yesterday. It was a two-second prayer so that I could let you know I did it, but it really was not from my heart." Feigned lips. Faking prayer. Pretending to care.

Unrepentant Prayer

Have you ever asked God for forgiveness, but you really had not repented? Oh, you sincerely wanted His forgiveness, but you had no intention of closing the door of opportunity for that same sin in the future. In your heart you still wanted to pamper that sin, but you were dealing with guilt about that sin. When we seek forgiveness without repentance we are speaking with feigned lips. Deceitful, false.

When we come before the throne, it is a serious time. We need to think about what we are saying and what we are requesting. Do we really want to see the answer to the prayer? Are we sincerely communicating with our God with open hearts and focused minds? Are we being honest?

Day 40
Just Judge (Psalm 17:2)

I remember one specific incident when I was a little girl. The back door of our house was in my bedroom. One night, my brother had a friend spend the night. The two boys decided to be mischievous and sneak out in the middle of the night to go to my cousin's house down the road. I was young and easily persuaded, so I sneaked out with them. Of course, my Dad caught us, and we got in trouble. He sent us back to bed and told us he would deal with all three of us in the morning. I was brokenhearted. I hated disappointing my Daddy.

Then the boys waited a little while and decided to try sneaking out again. They came through my room and went out the door. I stood at the door loudly whispering, "Boys, come back! You are going to get in trouble!" There I was standing at the open door when my Dad walked in the room. It looked like I was heading out with them. It looked really, really bad!

My Dad sent the other boy home and then made himself a pot of coffee. He said, "If I cannot get any sleep, neither will you." My Dad proceeded to make my brother and me stand at attention (Dad was a former Army drill sergeant) and lectured us the longest lecture I have ever heard in my whole life. We were so tired!

I was not guilty the second time, but I knew that my Dad was upset. I did not try to defend myself.

It was best I take the punishment.

Have you ever been accused of something you did not do? Have you ever been unjustly criticized or judged? Have you ever faced hardship that was not fair and was not your fault? David did.

Psalm 17:2 "Let my sentence come forth from thy presence; let thine eyes behold the things that are equal."

David did not try to defend himself to his accusers. He did not try to justify himself. David had a different mindset. He was more concerned with what God thought of him than what people thought.

"Let my sentence come forth. Let my verdict, my judgment, my justification come forth from Thy presence."

David wanted God's approval. He was not concerned with man's approval. He wanted God to fight the battle to justify him. He trusted God.

"... let thine eyes behold the things that are equal." God can see the truth. When man makes uninformed judgments, condemns without the facts, or slanders and injures our testimonies unjustly, God sees the truth. He sees what is right. He is not partial in His view. He is not a respecter of persons. He is not tainted by bias. He is a just judge.

David cried out, "Search me, God. If I have done something to deserve this, show me. If I have not, defend me." David did not take on the battle by himself. He went to the Just Judge who knows all things.

Are you fighting your battles of injustice? Are you more concerned about what man thinks than turning to the Just Judge?

Day 41
Purposed Mouth (Psalm 17:3)

Have you ever laid awake at night pondering a trial? Has sleep ever evaded you because you were spending time doing a heart inspection?

Throughout my life as a parent, I have faced this many times. Now that I have a child out on his own thousands of miles away, I have done this more than ever. Parenting a child who is transitioning into adulthood is difficult enough but doing it from a different continent is even tougher! I am not there with him to intervene when he is in trouble or if he makes a bad decision. I cannot hop on a plane and handle situations. I cannot sit down with him face-to-face and help him make right decisions. When he messes up or things do not go the way I hoped, sometimes I lie on my bed wide awake pondering the trial and inspecting my own heart.

David did the same thing as he faced his trials.

Psalm 17:3 "Thou hast proved mine heart; thou hast visited me in the night; thou hast tried me, and shalt find nothing; I am purposed that my mouth shall not transgress."

He was facing a dark time, and yet he knew that God was using this trial to prove him, to try him, and to refine him. As sleep escaped him, he laid on his bed searching his own heart. God visited with him in the night and helped in the inspection.

God searches the heart, and His search is more thorough than ours. Our hearts are deceptive and can fool us, but our hearts cannot fool God. As God tried David's heart and as David was party to the inspection process, David said his conscience was clear. This trial was not because of sin, neither had he sinned because of the trial, but there was one area David knew was a temptation. It was a temptation to sin with his lips.

With that in mind, David purposed firmly in his heart and mind that he would not cross that line. He would not give in to the temptation to complain. He would not allow his mouth to speak foolishly. He would not slander his enemy or charge God with being unjust in sending the trial. He had purposed that his mouth would not transgress throughout the duration of the trial.

Are you facing a trial?

1. Do not be afraid to inspect your heart to see if this trial was caused by sin in your life or to see if you have sinned in how you are dealing with the trial.
2. Submit to God's inspection of your heart and be ready to repent if He points out things in your heart that are not right with Him.
3. Embrace the trial knowing that God uses the fires of trials to prove us and refine us for His glory.
4. Purpose in your heart not to give into transgressing with your mouth through complaining, through speaking sinfully to

others or about others, or through sinful accusations against God.

Day 42
Two Paths (Psalm 17:4-6)

Here is an interesting fact: Several roads here have names, but most people do not know what they are. The people do not give directions by road names. They give directions by area names and then landmarks. If you looked on Google Maps or some form of GPS navigation, several roads would be labelled with names, but it would do you no good to mention those names to the average person or to a taxi driver. The roads, for the most part, are not labelled. There are a few directional road signs on main roads, but even those are a recent addition.

So how do we know we are on the right path? Honestly, we get on the wrong road quite often. When using GPS, sometimes it sends us to a road, but when we get there the road may simply be a footpath or may no longer exist. Getting around in this country is an adventure, and I guess that makes me all the more thankful that we have an adventurous nature.

But God does not want us to live life that way.

Psalm 17:4-6 "Concerning the works of men, by the word of thy lips I have kept me from the paths of the destroyer. Hold up my goings in thy paths, that my footsteps slip not. I have called upon thee, for thou wilt hear me, O God: incline thine ear unto me, and hear my speech."

There were two things David was counting on to keep him on the right path and away from the paths of the destroyer.

1) **God's Word**
   "... by the word of thy lips..."
2) **Prayer**
   "I have called upon thee..."

David did not depend on himself and his own wisdom to stay off the wrong path. That would be even less reliable than us using GPS in a third-world country! God's Word gives very clear instructions of how to stay on the right path and away from the path of the destroyer. The problem comes when we try to rely on our spiritual sense of direction. It also comes when we trust bad sources for direction.

Another interesting fact: When stopping to ask for directions here, we have to be prepared for wrong directions. In this culture, people want to be helpful insomuch that even if they do not know how to get somewhere, they will give you directions anyway just to be kind to you. They do not want to let you down. They want to give you an answer that will make you happy.

Psalm 1:1-2 "Blessed is the man that walketh not in the counsel of the ungodly, nor standeth in the way of sinners, nor sitteth in the seat of the scornful. But his delight is in the law of the LORD; and in his law doth he meditate day and night."

God warns us not to follow the directions of the ungodly. He tells us to call out to Him to help us navigate these roads in life. We must quit relying on our own understanding or the counsel of ungodly sources, and we must acknowledge His authority and His wisdom.

Proverbs 3:5-6 "Trust in the LORD with all thine heart; and lean not unto thine own understanding. In all thy ways acknowledge him, and he shall direct thy paths."

If we truly want to stay on the right path as we navigate through this life, it will show up in how frequently and diligently we get into God's Word and on our knees in prayer.

Day 43
Running Scared (Psalm 17:8-9)

Can I be honest about something? I usually try to stay very positive in my tone, but there is something on social media that drives me nuts. Occasionally in my news feed on social media, someone will post a meme or a quote that really frustrates me.

"Be the kind of woman that when your feet hit the floor each morning the devil says, 'Oh no! She is up!'"

Why does this quote drive me so crazy? It is based in pride and completely inaccurate. The devil is not one bit afraid of us. His knees are not knocking because of us. He is not worried at all about you or me. We are never spiritual enough that we intimidate the devil. We are never strong enough that he feels his courage melt away or feels his cause is hopeless. No, like the destroyer he is, he continues to seek to devour us, and he thoroughly enjoys the hunt.

What gets him frustrated? What foils his plans? What disappoints that lion seeking his prey?

Psalm 17:8-9 "Keep me as the apple of the eye, hide me under the shadow of thy wings, From the wicked that oppress me, from my deadly enemies, who compass me about."

The apple of his eye is not talking about a shiny piece of fruit God is adoring from His throne. The apple of the eye is a phrase that describes the pupil of the eye. It is the very center of the eye that we see through. When David said, "Keep me as the apple of the eye," he was asking God to keep Him in the center of His vision. He wanted God to keep a close, protective eye on Him and not to let anything else obstruct His watchful view of him. Not only did David want God to watch over him, He wanted God to hide Him. He wanted God to draw him close by and cover him in the safety that only God Himself can provide.

The devil is not afraid when you or I get up and feel like super-spiritual warriors. What puts him on the run is when we run under the shadow of the wings of God. When we submit to the Lord in our weakness, the devil's battle plans are hindered. That is why James 4:7 starts out the way it does. It begins with submitting.

James 4:7 "Submit yourselves therefore to God. Resist the devil, and he will flee from you."

As we serve in a place where the enemy is raging, it is not courage that will get me through. The enemies are swarming around us, and the dangers are growing. We are compassed about on every side. To be blunt, there are days when I have no courage.

I miss the freedoms I had in America to pass out tracts openly everywhere we went. I miss being able to strike up a conversation at any time about the Bible and spiritual things without worry of being turned in to the police. Sometimes we are seen as being full of courage and bravery. We are seen as great heroes. We certainly are not heroes, and courage is not my strength. Yes, I have fear sometimes. I do not like the thought of jail. I definitely do not relish the thought of my husband or children being in jail. The good thing is that this is not about my courage. It is not about my family's courage. It is about us running. It is about where we are running when we are afraid.

Where do we run for our comfort and protection? To whom do we call out? Do we wake up in the morning thinking, "Do not worry, God. I got this!" or do we run under His wings?

No, the devil is not worried when I get out of bed each morning, but I know the One who gives the devil pause.

Psalm 56:3 "What time I am afraid, I will trust in thee."

Day 44
His Sword and His Hand (Psalm 17:13-14)

We have the two most amazing dogs in the world. They are full of personality and purpose, and they bring us great pleasure. They have several jobs that they fulfill which means they are not just pets. They are part of our ministry here because they are part of our survival.

The German Shepherd is our Barney Fife guard dog. He takes his job seriously. No animal or person may enter our property without permission. There have been many times we have found bird feathers scattered around the property. Two cats have perished because of him. Dozens of rats have met their demise. Humans dare not attempt unlawful entrance. They will not even come close to the gate for fear of the big dog.

The little Japanese Spitz is our guardian from little things. She is quick to point out snakes. This is a handy skill because there is a large variety of venomous snakes here. She also protects us from ants, bees, caterpillars, and vicious birthday balloons. Her greatest talents are rescuing us from boredom with her crazy antics, licking away all dirt from our faces, and preventing us from ever feeling unloved.

They are outdoor dogs, but every now and then they get the treat of coming in the house for a few minutes. I, however, am very strict about their admission into my kitchen. Nasty dogs in clean kitchens where food is prepared does not set well with me.

On certain occasions, like when I drop an egg on the floor or when there is a large food spill, I sneak and let our dogs in the kitchen. They come running in thinking that they are getting away with being bad. As they slurp up the gooey mess that I do not want to have clean myself, they feel like criminals evading my judicious eyes. They do not suspect for a moment that they are actually accomplishing my will. In their minds, they are Bonnie and Clyde on a criminal spree stealing treasures from the kitchen floor before the police surround them and whisk them off to puppy jail outside.

Psalm 17:13-14 "Arise, O LORD,
disappoint him, cast him down: deliver
my soul from the wicked, which is thy
sword: From men which are thy hand, O
LORD, from men of the world..."

Wait, the wicked are God's sword? Men of the world are His hand?

Yes, God is in complete control even when it seems like the enemy is approaching victory. In reality, God is merely using them to accomplish a greater purpose, just like me using my canine Bonnie and Clyde to accomplish my purpose. Many times in the Bible, God used wicked nations to chastise His people. His people would rebel against Him and turn to other gods, so the Lord would bring Israel into captivity under other nations. He did that in order to bring Israel back to Him. Those other nations were His sword, and they never knew it.

I think of when the devil approached God about Job. The devil surely thought he was the victor as he took away Job's family, possessions, and health. God, however, was allowing Satan to be His hand in shaping and molding Job. Job was a mature and upright man, but there was one area God wanted to refine. The Lord used the enemy as part of the plan.

In this Psalm, David acknowledged God's complete sovereignty. The Lord is in control even over the enemy. He uses them as His sword of judgment and chastisement. He also uses them as His potter's hand to shape and mold His people.

Are you facing the enemy? Maybe it is the Lord using the enemy as His sword and His hand. Recognize God's sovereignty. He is in control. Call out to Him and trust His greater purposes in your trials

Day 45
Their Portion (Psalm 17:14-15)

We stepped out of the church and saw him. He was sitting in his rickshaw and resting. Our scooter and motorcycle were parked right beside him, so as we were putting on our helmets and loading our things into the scooter seat we began talking with the rickshaw driver.

He was all smiles and full of pleasantness. Then he asked where we had been. My husband told him we had just left church and that we were Christians. Suddenly the man's demeanor changed drastically. He started speaking rapidly, and we had a difficult time understanding him. We could only catch a few words here and there.

One of those words was yuddha. My husband thought he said yahudi which means Jew. He was not sure why this man was talking about a Jew, but since the communication seemed to be hindered, my husband pulled out a tract and handed it to the man. The man angrily grabbed the tract, pretended to use it as toilet paper on his backside (above the clothing thankfully), and then threw the tract on the ground.

It became clear at that point that the man was not pro-Christian. The man then proceeded to use his limited English skills. Unfortunately it was a single word that I would never speak, much less type!

My husband picked up the tract, put it in his pocket. We then got on our two-wheelers and drove off. I was glad my husband handled the situation calmly.

When we stopped for lunch, my husband explained that he thought the man said yahudi (Jew). When I said he had said yuddha, we finally figured out what he was saying. Yuddha means war.

It would be easy to get angry with the man, but there is a truth that makes me pity him. It is a truth that keeps me focused on my purpose and goal. It restrains me from responding to persecution the wrong way.

Psalm 17:14 "From men which are thy hand, O LORD, from men of the world, which have their portion in this life, and whose belly thou fillest with thy hid treasure: they are full of children, and leave the rest of their substance to their babes."

The angry rickshaw driver has his portion in this life. Whatever blessings come his way in this life, that is the best he can ever hope to have. What if that rickshaw driver suddenly received a fancy car, a nice house, and stylish modern clothing? That would be the best he could ever have. What if he was given money, fame, and possessions that he could pass down to his children and his grandchildren? When he dies, whatever he has gets passed on to others. As for him, his portion-- his blessing-- is finished. It is over.

That rickshaw driver did not have fancy things, cars, and a nice house. He had a ratty, rundown old rickshaw. His clothes were dirty. He was thin and looked aged well beyond his actual years. It breaks my heart even years later to think of him. Without Christ, that ratty old rickshaw is all he will ever hope to enjoy. When his life is finished, his portion is finished. His true suffering will begin.

As I look around me, I see rich people and I see poor people. I see happy faces and I see suffering faces. I see those who enjoy our company and those who wish us harm. All have been blessed by the hand of God in some fashion. Some have been blessed more than others, but they all have one thing in common. No matter what they have in this life, if they do not know Christ, that is their portion. That is the best they can hope for. When their life is over, the blessings will end. Their things will be passed on to their children, but they will enter eternity without hope. Dwelling on this truth keeps me from being bitter or angry. It makes me sad for them. It makes me not want to give up on them. It makes me want to keep sharing the Gospel with them.

I also dwell on another truth.

Psalm 17:15 "As for me, I will behold thy face in righteousness: I shall be satisfied, when I awake, with thy likeness."

No matter how difficult things get here on earth for me, I have hope. No matter how rich I am or how poor I am, no matter how sick I may be or if I live in health, no matter how much I struggle or how much I succeed, no matter how much persecution I face or how much loss I endure here in this life, when this life is over, I will stand before my Saviour in His righteousness and behold His face. I will open my eyes and be satisfied as I gaze upon His countenance.

Read it again and let it sink in:

Psalm 17:15 "As for me, I will behold thy face in righteousness: I shall be satisfied, when I awake, with thy likeness."

The enemies that surround us have their portion in this life, but those of us who are clothed in the righteousness of Christ will receive our portion and satisfaction the moment we open our eyes after death. It will be worth it all.

Day 46
Racing Past Treasures (Psalm 18:1)

My daughter and I love to run. We love one mile sprints; we love running 5k's; we even love running 10k's. We both aspire to work up to a half marathon as our next goal. When we visit the States, we hope to enter some races-- not that we would win anything, but it would be fun.

I can just see us now. We enter into a 5k race. On the day of the race, everyone lines up at the starting line except us. We decide we will line up twenty yards ahead of everyone else. (After all, how important is that starting line anyway?) Then I can see a race official approaching us and making us go back to the beginning. "You cannot run this race unless you start at the right place."

What does this have to do with Psalm 18? I almost messed up this morning. I almost missed a great treasure. By the grace of God, the Spirit drew me back to the beginning.

I sat down to read the Psalm and quickly brushed past the introduction to the Psalm.

"To the chief musician... blah blah blah... David wrote it... that is good to know... during the time of Saul chasing him... okay, got it. Now on to the meat of the Psalm."

I read the whole Psalm. There were good things in it, but it was like there was something missing. The Psalm spoke of God's power and His provision in times of trouble. Those things are good and true, but I missed the most important part and did not even realize it.

Do you realize that every word of God is pure, and that all scripture is inspired by God?

2 Timothy 3:16-17 "All scripture is given by inspiration of God, and is profitable for doctrine, for reproof, for correction, for instruction in righteousness: That the man of God may be perfect, throughly furnished unto all good works."

It is all important and valuable. Even the introductory titles in Psalms matter. I had tried to skip the starting line and jumped straight into the race. The Race Official, the Holy Spirit, brought me back to the beginning and showed me that the starting line matters. In this Psalm, everything that follows is based on some facts revealed in the title and description. In my haste and in my devaluing of God's Word, I flew past the source from which the rest of the Psalm flows.

Psalm 18:1 "To the chief Musician, A Psalm of David, the servant of the LORD, who spake unto the LORD the words of this song in the day that the LORD delivered him from the hand of all his enemies, and from the hand of Saul: And he said, I will love thee, O LORD, my strength."

A Psalm of David, the servant of the LORD.

Why did David get to experience such intimacy with the Lord? Why did God so tenderly protect David? Why did God deliver David from the hand of his enemies time after time? David was the servant of the LORD. David had laid his life down on the altar before God. He did not live life for himself. He died to self.

Galatians 2:20 "I am crucified with Christ: nevertheless I live; yet not I, but Christ liveth in me: and the life which I now live in the flesh I live by the faith of the Son of God, who loved me, and gave himself for me."

1 Corinthians 6:19 "What? know ye not that your body is the temple of the Holy Ghost which is in you, which ye have of God, and ye are not your own? For ye are bought with a price: therefore glorify God in your body, and in your spirit, which are God's."

Romans 12:1 "I beseech you therefore, brethren, by the mercies of God, that ye present your bodies a living sacrifice, holy, acceptable unto God, which is your reasonable service."

Luke 9:23 "And he said to them all, If any man will come after me, let him deny himself, and take up his cross daily, and follow me."

What about me? How did I plan my day today? Did it look like a servant following, or did it look like a master leading? Did I plan to serve self today, or did I lay my life on the altar today?

"... I will love thee, O LORD..."

David's protector was also David's love. David was devoted to His God because he loved the Lord. They had a rich intimacy.

Do I have that rich intimacy and devotion? Am I pursuing it daily? Am I settling for less?

"... my strength."

David acknowledged he was nothing without God. He needed the Lord. Without the Lord, David could do nothing. He was completely dependent. He did not rely on his cunning or his battle skills. He did not rely on himself. God was his strength.

Do I try to do things in my own power and strength? Do I realize just how desperately I need the Lord every minute of the day?

The heart of a servant, love and devotion, and a total dependency upon his God is the source from which everything in the rest of this Psalm flows. Those are also the things that are needed for me to experience the level of closeness David had with his Rock, his Fortress, his Deliverer. I almost missed it.

Note to self: The starting line matters.

Day 47
Redefining Worry (Psalm 18:2)

When I was in Bible college, one of the professors taught us an invaluable skill. He taught us that when we share the Gospel, we should try to define our words so that the person we are speaking to understands exactly what we mean. Sometimes people use the same words, but they have a different definition in their mind than the Bible definition.

For example, the words sin and holiness are very distorted in the country where my family lives. Sin to them is doing things that are extremely bad and malicious. It is things that go against the society or culture and would have you looked upon as a criminal. To them, sin would be things like murder and mutilation, killing a cow, or being a corrupt government official. Stealing when you have a need, lying, or cheating would not be sins because they could help you. It would only be bad if you got caught and your neighbors were upset with you. They are deeply concerned with what their neighbors think of them!

These things are not the Bible definition of sin. The Bible definition of sin is anything that goes against God's Word. It is things that go against His laws. In order for me to share the Gospel, I have to make sure the other person and I have the same definitions in mind.

I now have the habit if constantly looking up definitions. Here is a definition for you:

WORRY: to feel or experience concern or anxiety, fret

In Psalm 18, David had every reason to be worried, but he was not. He was surrounded by the threat of death. Death itself was a snare around him. (vs 4-5) He was in distress. (vs 6) Things did not look good! Why was not he consumed with worry? He had a proper view of his God.

Psalm 18:2 "The LORD is my rock, and my fortress, and my deliverer; my God, my strength, in whom I will trust; my buckler, and the horn of my salvation, and my high tower."

David's enemies were stronger than him! He was outnumbered, and he was afraid. So why was not he engulfed in worry?

Psalm 18:17 "... for they were too strong for me."

Psalm 18:4 "... the floods of ungodly men made me afraid."

He knew the men were strong, but His God was stronger. He knew instead of wallowing in worry he should call to his Creator. He knew his God would hear him.

Psalm 18:6 "In my distress I called upon the LORD, and cried unto my God: he

heard my voice out of his temple, and my
cry came before him, even into his ears."

And God heard! David then gives a beautiful word display of the might and fierceness of the Lord. The earth shaking and trembling because of God's wrath, the heavens being bowed, thundering and lightning, the blast of the breath of His nostrils...

God delivered! Our God is *that* big! He is *that* strong! When our problems seem to surround us and overtake us, we need to be reminded how big our God is. Our problems may be big, but our God is infinitely bigger.

I have heard the statement:

"Do not tell God how big your problems
are. Tell your problems how big your God
is."

I have a better idea. Do both! Call out to God. Tell Him how big your problems are. He wants us to call to Him like David did. After that, tell Him you know He is bigger than your problems. Put your confidence in His strength. Yes, the problems are too big for you and me, but they are never too big for our Creator.

So maybe we should redefine the word worry.

WORRY: Having too small of a view of our Heavenly Father.

Day 48
Go Wash Your Hands (Psalm 18:20)

I am not one to go digging in dirt. When working in flowerbeds, I like to use gloves. I do not like to get mud and dirt all over my hands. When my hands get dirty, I can literally feel the soil drying on my hands. It drives me crazy. I have to wash my hands several times a day. But my boys?

Boys are dirt magnets. My younger son can get dirty from head to toe in a matter of minutes. Though I can feel dirt drying on my hands, my youngest child can have a mound of dirt on him and never feel a thing. He sits down at the dinner table and Daddy always asks, "Did you wash your hands?"

As my son holds up his hands for inspection, the grime glares. I am left wondering, did he really have to look at his hands to know that they had enough dirt on them to bury a full-sized car? Of course, he is told to get up and go wash his hands before sitting down to eat.

Psalm 18:20 "The LORD rewarded me
according to my righteousness;
according to the cleanness of my hands
hath he recompensed me."

David hated dirty hands, too. He loved righteousness. This is not talking about him having his own righteousness for salvation. None of us have that!

Romans 3:10 "As it is written, There is
none righteous, no, not one:"

That kind of righteousness is imputed to us at salvation. We receive the righteousness of Christ.

The righteousness David is talking about is not salvation righteousness. This righteousness is daily right living. This righteousness is keeping his hands out of muck of sin and following God's Word. This righteousness is daily separation and a pure walk. He did a hand inspection in the middle of his trial and found that his hands were clean. This trail he faced was not the results of sin.

When we face a trial, it is wise for us to do a hand inspection. Sometimes our trials are a result of sin and living contrary to God's Word. For example, imagine a couple facing a financial struggle. They call out to God for help, but it seems He is not hearing. They sit down with their pastor for counsel. The pastor starts asking some tough questions to help them do a hand inspection. He asks them about how they spend their money, if they budget, if they tithe faithfully, and if they are wise stewards with their finances. As the inspection continues, they realize that the majority of the financial struggle was caused by unwise choices, including forsaking tithing and making foolish purchases.

They were expecting God to be their rock, fortress, and deliverer while having dirty hands. God deals with His children according to the cleanness of their hands.

Psalm 18:24-26 "Therefore hath the LORD recompensed me according to my righteousness, according to the cleanness of my hands in his eyesight. With the merciful thou wilt shew thyself merciful; with an upright man thou wilt shew thyself upright; With the pure thou wilt shew thyself pure; and with the froward thou wilt shew thyself froward."

Here is some good news: If you do a hand inspection and find you have dirty hands in your trial, God shows us how to wash our hands. It is inevitable at times that we will find we have dirty hands. David also had times when he realized his hands were dirty. (Psalm 51) When we find we have our hands dirtied by sin, here is how we wash them:

1 John 1:9 "If we confess our sins, he is faithful and just to forgive us our sins, and to cleanse us from all unrighteousness."

Proverbs 28:13 "He that covereth his sins shall not prosper: but whoso confesseth and forsaketh them shall have mercy."

Are you facing a trial? Take a moment to inspect your hands using the Word of God as your magnifying glass. If you find you have clean hands, then trust that God will deal with you accordingly. If you find your hands are dirty repent, confess, and forsake the sin. Wash your hands in His forgiveness.

Day 49
Without Excuse (Psalm 19:1)

Sometimes at night I sit on the front porch and gaze up at the stars. They glisten and flicker. They are a mesmerizing part of creation. They loudly declare the power and glory of my God, the Creator.

Psalm 19:1 "The heavens declare the glory of God; and the firmament sheweth his handywork."

It is amazing to me to think that as I look up at the stars, it will not be long until my family on the other side of the world will be able to look up at the sky and see the same display of beauty and wonder. I picture in my mind my older son, my mom, and my grandmother looking up at the night sky just as I do.

I also picture something else. That same night sky can be seen all over the world. It can be seen in the jungles of Africa. It can be seen in North Korea. It can be seen in the Arctic and in the Pacific Islands. They may have a slightly different view of stars than me, but the stars are there. The moon is there. Everyone has the same opportunity to see the creative work of God on display.

"What about the people in the jungles of Africa who have never heard of the name Jesus? How can they be judged?"

They look up at the night sky and they have a choice. They can respond to that display and say,

"Someone created that. I want to know who," or they can create their own truth and reject the light God has given them. They can worship creation or create their own version of a god, or they can acknowledge what their eyes see-- that Someone bigger and greater than them created all things with beauty and perfect order. These things did not happen by accident.

When we respond to the light God gives us, He gives more light. For the tribal people in the jungles who reject making creation their god and they reject the notion that they can create their own gods, He sends a missionary. He pricks the heart of someone to go to a strange place.

God is not willing that any should perish. He wants everyone to be saved, even people in remote places. We all have the same responsibility: to respond to the light that God gives us. When we see creation, the Spirit whispers in our hearts, "You did not make this. I did. This did not happen by chance." Are we going to respond in faith?

The heavens are like the first page of a Gospel tract. If we read it and hunger for the second page, God will send the second page. If we read that first page and reject the truth it declares, then we have rejected God.

Day 50
Cliffhanger (Psalm 19:7-10)

True confession: I do not like cliffhangers. I do not like reading books and getting to the end, only to realize that the book ends with a cliffhanger. I do not like watching shows that end each episode with a cliffhanger.

Cliffhanger: (noun) The ending of an episode of a series drama that leaves the audience in suspense.

Why do I hate cliffhangers? I like resolution. I like to know how things turn out. I do not want to wait until next week to find out if Marco took the bribe or if Bubba healed from his gator bite or if the missionary escaped the angry mob. I want to know now. Today.

As a writer, I love writing cliffhangers. They keep people hooked! I just do not like being on the receiving end of a suspenseful ending.

Psalm 19 is like a five-page Gospel tract. There is no cliffhanger there. God, through David, gives the story from beginning to end.

The first page of the tract is an introduction to the marvelous Creator. His story is declared through His creation.

Psalm 19:2 "Day unto day uttereth speech, and night unto night sheweth knowledge."

Every day and every night, we can look around us and see that there is a God who created all the beauty, wonder, and magnificence that we see around us. Creation is the first page of that Gospel tract, but what if you stopped there? Is seeing creation and acknowledging there is a Creator enough for salvation? No, it is not. Unfortunately, that is where many people fall short.

"I believe in God," they declare. That is good, but it is not enough. Even the devils believe.

James 2:19 "Thou believest that there is one God; thou doest well: the devils also believe, and tremble."

If a person stops at "I believe in God" or even "I believe in Jesus," it is like they read a chapter in a book and did not finish the rest of the story. They ended on a cliffhanger and there is no resolution of the dilemma.

So, now we are on page number two of the Gospel tract. David suddenly switches from speaking of creation and how it declares the wonderful Creator (19:1-6) to talking about God's Word (19:7-10). He does this because it is impossible to be saved apart from God's Word, and it is impossible to know the Creator apart from God's Word.

Romans 10:17 "So then faith cometh by hearing, and hearing by the word of God."

Psalm 19:7 "The law of the LORD is
perfect, converting the soul..."

His Word is perfect. His Word is sure. His Word is right. His Word is pure. It is clean and true and righteous. It changes us. It makes us wise. It gives joy. It opens our eyes. It is eternal. God's Word is more precious than any substance this world has to offer.

Psalm 19:10 "More to be desired are
they than gold, yea, than much fine gold:
sweeter also than honey and the
honeycomb."

His Word is absolutely critical for salvation. What if a person believes in God and believes God's Word is true? Is that enough for salvation? Those things certainly are vital, but is that enough?

As much as I dislike cliffhangers... (Well, at least I will give you a hint: This Psalm 19 Gospel tract is five pages long, and we have only talked about page one and two.)

Day 51
Check Your Measuring Stick (Psalm 19:11)

I was sitting in Missions class in Bible college. The professor was explaining the term repentance in Scripture. As he continued teaching God's Word, the Spirit was doing a work in my heart. I realized I was not saved. I had never repented of my sin, and I felt the weight of conviction bearing down on my shoulders and gripping my heart.

A few years ago, a friend pulled me to the side privately after church and did something I did not really like. It was uncomfortable. It was embarrassing. It was, however, necessary. She pointed out something I was doing that was not wise. Correction was followed by conviction from the Holy Spirit.

Just a few months ago, another friend a private message. Again, correction. Reproof. My flesh did not like it. It wanted to defend and get angry, but I kept reminding myself she is a friend. She was not being mean. She cared about me. As I took time over the following days to reflect on her words, the Lord pointed out some things in my heart and actions that did not please Him. Conviction.

Last month I went on a bicycle ride. I popped my earbuds in my ears and turned on a sermon to stream on my phone as I rode. As I listened to the sermon-- conviction. The Holy Spirit took the Word of God and aimed it at my heart.

Psalm 19:11 "Moreover by them is thy
servant warned: and in keeping of them
there is great reward."

Moreover by God's Word (law, statutes, testimony, commandment, fear, judgments) we are warned. God's Word confronts our sin. The Holy Spirit takes that Word and convicts.

John 16:7-8 "Nevertheless I tell you the
truth; It is expedient for you that I go
away: for if I go not away, the Comforter
will not come unto you; but if I depart, I
will send him unto you. And when he is
come, he will reprove the world of sin,
and of righteousness, and of judgment:"

Conviction. Our flesh hates it. When we are confronted, we want to find fault in the messenger. Names like Pharisee and legalist start popping up in our minds. Phrases like "You are so judgmental" roll off our lips. It seems that our measuring stick to decide if something is true is if we agree with it or if we like it. If it offends us, then the messenger must therefore be a Pharisee judging me.

Conviction is the third page of the Psalm 19 Gospel tract. Without conviction of the Holy Spirit, a person cannot be saved. Without being confronted about sin and seeing ourselves as sinners, we would be destined to die in those sins. We would never even know that we needed a Saviour.

Should the measuring stick of truth be how we feel? Should our measuring stick be whether or not we are offended? If that were the case, we would be in trouble, because the Gospel itself is offensive.

The measuring stick of truth is God's Word. When we are confronted, if we will take the time to check God's Word and inspect our hearts in light of God's Word, it is quite possible that what we are dealing with is not being offended, but instead conviction from the Holy Spirit.

The next time you are confronted by something or someone, do not react immediately. Take time to search the Bible to see if what the messenger is saying is true. If you are offended by what the messenger said, do not allow that offence to dictate whether the message was true or not. Allow God's Word to be the measuring stick of truth. Then respond to how the Spirit works in your heart based on God's Word. You just may find that the messenger is a faithful friend who simply cares enough about you to confront you.

Proverbs 27:6 "Faithful are the wounds
of a friend; but the kisses of an enemy
are deceitful."

Day 52
The Progression (Psalm 19:12-13)

Psalm 19 is an amazing Gospel tract broken into five parts. All five parts are necessary for salvation.

Page 1- An acknowledging of the Creator, God
Page 2- God's Word which confronts us about God's holiness and our sin
Page 3- Conviction of the Holy Spirit, where the Spirit takes the Word of God and shows us as sinners needing a Saviour
Page 4- Repentance

Psalm 19:12 "Who can understand his errors? cleanse thou me from secret faults. Keep back thy servant also from presumptuous sins; let them not have dominion over me: then shall I be upright, and I shall be innocent from the great transgression."

David not only acknowledged he was a sinner, but he rejected his sin. He turned from it! Repentance is a change of mind that produces a change in the direction we face. Whereas we were once turned toward sin, embracing it, and loving it, repentance is when sin becomes ugly, vile, and dirty in our eyes. That ugliness will cause a change in direction. When we were once turned toward sin in our affections, we then turn toward God instead. It is a humbling that causes us to seek God's forgiveness, because He is holy and we are not. We realize we are the enemies of God, yet no longer desire to be His enemy. We call out to Him in repentance, "Cleanse me! Free me from the bondage of sin!"

David admitted that God must do the work. God must cleanse. God must break him free from the dominion of sin. We, too, must understand we cannot cleanse ourselves. We cannot break free. We will never be good enough or do enough good to earn salvation. Jesus paid for our sins, was buried, and rose again victorious so that we could have a way to be forgiven. He died in our place. We must repent, confess, and turn to Him.

Acts 3:19 "Repent ye therefore, and be converted, that your sins may be blotted out..."

For those of us who are saved, there is also a warning about sin. It has a progression if we do not deal with it. David admitted **secret sin**. Then he asked God to keep him back from **presumptuous sin**. That is sin that is proud, open, and arrogant with no shame. Then there is **great transgression**. There are some sins that go so far as to impact us for the rest of our lives. There are some sins that disqualify us from serving God in certain areas. There are some sins that mar our testimony so deeply that we are rendered ineffective for Christ. There is also a continuing in sin that God gives warning that we can cross the line-- sin unto death. If we do not deal with secret sins, they will develop into presumptuous sins. When we do not repent, the sin can turn into great transgression.

Revelation 3:19 "As many as I love, I rebuke and chasten: be zealous therefore, and repent."

Day 53
Misunderstood (Psalm 19:12)

Her name was Dilmaya. I met her in the streets. As she passed by I gave her the standard cultural greeting for non-Christians, and she replied back with the Christian greeting. I was surprised and asked her, "Oh, you are a believer?"

She smiled a huge grin, and the elderly woman affirmed that she was a Christian. She invited me to her home. I went to visit with her one day and brought a friend to aid me in translation. As we began talking with Dilmaya, we asked her to tell us her salvation story. She said that she needed physical healing, and her gods were not able to heal so she went to a Christian church one day. The leader of the church led her in a prayer that she repeated after him, and then he declared her to be a Christian. That was two years prior to this.

As my friend and I continued talking with her, it became clear Dilmaya had never heard the Gospel. As we talked about Jesus dying for her sin, confusion swept across her face. She had never heard these things before.

We see things like this all the time here. The people visit a charismatic church in hopes of healing, financial blessing, or getting a problem solved. The charismatic pastor has them repeat some prayer and then declares them Christians. All the while, the Gospel is neglected and the people are still trapped in their greatest problem, the problem of sin.

Our Gospel Tract in 5 Pages from Psalm 19:
Page 1- An acknowledging of the Creator, God (vs. 1-6)
Page 2- God's Word which confronts us about God's holiness and our sin (vs. 7-10)
Page 3- Conviction of the Holy Spirit, where the Spirit takes the Word of God and shows us as sinners needing a Saviour (vs. 11)
Page 4- Repentance (vs. 12)
Page 5- Understanding and calling out in faith.

Psalm 19:12 "Who can understand his errors? cleanse thou me..."

The step of understanding and calling out in faith has been distorted in modern Christian evangelism. In our pursuit of numbers we want "calling out." We pursue it even to the neglect of understanding of the Gospel and the necessity of faith.

How is this great neglect carried out? It is often seen in the "repeat this prayer" practice. A person who does not understand the Gospel can still repeat a prayer with no problem. (Trust me! I did it!) Then that person spends the rest of her life trusting in a prayer instead of trusting in Christ's finished work on the cross. Her salvation is based on the work of a prayer instead of the grace of God.

It is vital that when we present the Gospel, we do not rush too quickly to the calling out part. We do not want simply calling out. We want calling out in faith.

Ephesians 2:8-9 "For by grace are ye saved through faith; and that not of yourselves: it is the gift of God: Not of works, lest any man should boast."

Romans 10:13-15, 17 "For whosoever shall call upon the name of the Lord shall be saved. How then shall they call on him in whom they have not believed? and how shall they believe in him of whom they have not heard? and how shall they hear without a preacher? And how shall they preach, except they be sent? as it is written, How beautiful are the feet of them that preach the gospel of peace, and bring glad tidings of good things! So then faith cometh by hearing, and hearing by the word of God."

What must they understand?

God is holy and righteous, and they are not.

Romans 3:10-11 "As it is written, There is none righteous, no, not one: There is none that understandeth, there is none that seeketh after God."

They are sinners who have transgressed against God's law.

Romans 3:23 "For all have sinned, and come short of the glory of God;"

They deserve God's judgment for sin, which is death.

> *Romans 6:23 "For the wages of sin is death..."*

But Jesus, the holy Son of God, took their place of death and died on the cross.

> *Romans 6:23 "For the wages of sin is death; but the gift of God is eternal life through Jesus Christ our Lord."*

They must repent and turn to God.

> *Acts 17:30 "... but now commandeth all men every where to repent:"*

They must call out in faith, believing that Jesus died for them, was buried, and rose again because He is God.

> *Romans 10:9 "That if thou shalt confess with thy mouth the Lord Jesus, and shalt believe in thine heart that God hath raised him from the dead, thou shalt be saved."*

They must trust that calling out in faith is their only means of forgiveness of sin.

> *Romans 10:13 "For whosoever shall call upon the name of the Lord shall be saved."*

If they understand these things, they will not need a repeat-a-prayer moment. They will know to call out to God from their heart to seek His forgiveness for sin, trusting that Jesus is their only means of salvation. If the Spirit is convincing them of sin and convicting them of sin, they will not need us to twist their arm, coerce them, manipulate them, or beg them. We do not want big numbers of professing Christians. We want people truly calling out to God for salvation in faith.

Be patient in presenting the Gospel. Wait for the Spirit to open their eyes of understanding, to convince them of their sinful state, and to draw them to God.

Day 54
Keep the Change (Psalm 19:14)

I love a good sale. Sales are rare here, and I miss them. Good sales are so rare that when I find one, I post about it on social media! Last week there was a "buy one get one free" sale on facial tissues. I could not believe it! Usually the idea of a sale here is six cents off the regular price. Six cents. Really.

One of my favorite types of sales in the States is after-holiday sales. Everything before the holiday is pricey, but the day after the holiday is a smorgasbord of discounted items. It makes me squeal with delight to see 70% off or more. I simply save the items for the next year. What a difference it makes after the holiday is over!

Unfortunately, we have taken this discount mentality into spiritual realms as well. After salvation, we have created this day-after-salvation discount Christianity. We get a true bargain with salvation and we celebrate it, but after salvation Christianity has been marked down 70%, 80%, 90% off. What a bargain! No sacrifice! Cheap and easy! There is a problem with this thinking.

Psalm 19:14 "Let the words of my mouth, and the meditation of my heart, be acceptable in thy sight, O LORD, my strength, and my redeemer."

When a person is truly saved, there is a change. One of those changes is a new desire to please God and a hatred for sin.

David wanted his words (the things that people can observe) and the meditations of his heart (things only God can observe) to please his Redeemer. David was not perfect, but that desire and pursuit to please his God was present.

If a person who professes salvation can still live, act, think, and do things just as he or she did before salvation without thought of pleasing God and without conviction for sin, there is a problem.

2 Corinthians 5:17 "Therefore if any man be in Christ, he is a new creature: old things are passed away; behold, all things are become new."

The old creature loved and embraced sin. The old creature lived for self, but the new creature has changed. When the new creature sins, there is conviction. The new creature has the Spirit of God dwelling inside producing fruit.

Galatians 5:22 "But the fruit of the Spirit is love, joy, peace, longsuffering, gentleness, goodness, faith, Meekness, temperance: against such there is no law."

As one of my favorite preachers has said, "When you get something as big as God living inside you, He is got to stick out somewhere!"

I have heard the statement, "Christians are not perfect, just forgiven." That is true, but there is a difference in a true born-again believer. They have a desire to please God, and sin does not hold the beauty it once did in their eyes.

Salvation is more than just a "get out of jail free" card. It produces a new creature. True salvation puts the person on a new path.

Day 55
Mrs. Fix-it And Her Horse and Chariot (Psalm 20)

I must admit it. I have been guilty. A crisis comes along, and out comes Mrs. Fix-it. You know her. You have been Mrs. Fix-it, too. Mrs. Fix-it is ready, willing, and able to solve all the problems of the world. She rides in with her horse and chariot with all the solutions and answers.

Sickness? She whips out medicines. Financial struggles? She starts planning and devising yard sales and money-making schemes. Marital problems? She is ready to counsel. When her children or husband or neighbors have problems? She can ride her horse and chariot to the rescue, ready for the battle.

She wants to solve everyone's problems, including her own. Psalm 20 is a strong and beautiful reminder that trusting in Mrs. Fix-it and her horses and chariots is dangerous.

Psalm 20:7 "Some trust in chariots, and some in horses: but we will remember the name of the LORD our God."

Chariots and horses seem like a great idea for a battle. They are strong and powerful. They can plow down infantry in minutes. David warned us not to trust in those things. He was writing to the chief musician who apparently was in a battle. David was reminding the chief musician where real hope and strength comes for battles. They come from the Lord.

Psalm 20:1-4 "To the chief Musician, A Psalm of David. The LORD hear thee in the day of trouble; the name of the God of Jacob defend thee; Send thee help from the sanctuary, and strengthen thee out of Zion; Remember all thy offerings, and accept thy burnt sacrifice; Selah. Grant thee according to thine own heart, and fulfil all thy counsel."

He reminds the musician that:

1. The Lord hears
2. The Lord defends
3. The Lord sends help
4. The Lord strengthens
5. The Lord remembers our devotion to Him
6. The Lord accepts our sacrifice of worship and prayer

Then David reminds the chief musician where his trust should be. Instead of jumping on the horse and chariot, get on your knees! God sees your heart, knows your needs, and hears your prayers. David's prayer was for his friend's prayers to be heard and answered. He was letting the musician know he was also with him in the battle through prayer. ("Grant thee... and fulfil...") David was saying, "I am praying that the Lord will give you your heart's desire and answer your prayers." Then David shows his faith in his God.

Psalm 20:5 "We will rejoice in thy salvation, and in the name of our God we will set up our banners: the LORD fulfil all thy petitions."

He says, "When God answers your prayer and saves you from this battle, we are going to celebrate! It will be a big party in God's name with flags and everything!"

David then reminded his friend what happens to those who trust in horses and chariots, and, in contrast, the condition of those who trust in the Lord.

Psalm 20:8 "They are brought down and fallen: but we are risen, and stand upright."

It is not that "horses and chariots" are bad. What is bad is that Mrs. Fix-it trusts in horses and chariots rather than in calling out to God. Mrs. Fix-it grabs the horse and chariot before even checking to see what God wants her to do in the situation. Mrs. Fix-it trusts her own plans and her own solutions rather than trusting in the Lord's plan.

Proverbs 3:5-6 "Trust in the LORD with all thine heart; and lean not unto thine own understanding. In all thy ways acknowledge him, and he shall direct thy paths."

Day 56
Do Not Miss the Point (Psalm 21)

There is a nasty habit that creeps into ministry circles. Sometimes we miss "the point." I have done it. Sometimes I have done it inwardly. Sometimes it was blatant and open for all to see. Sometimes it even looked and sounded spiritual, but there is nothing spiritual about missing "the point."

What exactly is "the point"? David nailed "the point." Here it is:

> Psalm 21:1 "The king shall joy in thy
> strength, O LORD; and in thy salvation
> how greatly shall he rejoice!"

Do you see "the point"? David was proclaiming salvation, victory over enemies, blessings, and majesty, but look where he pointed to give glory and credit. He did not point to self. He pointed to the true victor, his God. David's joy was not in his great accomplishments. He rejoiced because he knew that God did it, and that without God he was nothing. Look where David points:

Psalm 21:2 "Thou hast given..."
Psalm 21:3 "For thou preventest... thou settest..."
Psalm 21:4 "... thou gavest..."
Psalm 21:5 "... thy salvation..."
Psalm 21:6 "... thou hast made..."
Psalm 21:7 "... through the mercy of the most High..."
Psalm 21:8 "Thine hand..."

When we point to self, we are exalted in pride. We are also deluded in thinking that we can do anything apart from God's grace, strength, and power. What does missing "the point" look like?

- "I led him to the Lord."
- "I taught a great Sunday school class last week."
- "I passed out 300 tracts."
- "I... I... I..."

When we boast of self and point to our accomplishments or our victories, we miss the opportunity to give credit where it is due. We miss pointing to Him, our Strength, our Hope, our Guide, our Sustainer. He works in and through us. Without Him we can do nothing (John 15:5). (Oh, how guilty I am of this!)

When we learn to point in the right direction, we will have joy. We will also learn how to praise Him.

Psalm 21:13 "Be thou exalted, LORD, in thine own strength: so will we sing and praise thy power."

Day 57
The Game (Psalm 22)

Our family loves to play games. We play all sorts of games. Uno, Ticket to Ride, Catan, Phase 10, Risk, Pictionary-- we have quite a collection, and we are always looking for the next game to add to that collection.

One game we occasionally play is Monopoly. My youngest child has never been great at this game, because he cannot quite grasp the value of things in the game. He is known for selling a green property for $200 or trading Marvin Gardens so he can get Connecticut Avenue. He cannot comprehend why no one wants to buy the "Get Out of Jail Free" card for $75.

My oldest child loves to take advantage of this lack of understanding. He will make a ridiculously low offer for something, and I usually intercede. When I advise the younger boy on a fair trade, the oldest boy goes nuts. He misses out on a good deal.

Yes, I must admit just the other day we played, and I bought a property from the youngest child for much less than it was worth. At the urging of my husband and the weight of my own conscience, I gave my son a hefty tip to go with the purchase. My husband still says it was not enough, but let me talk about a deal much greater than a Monopoly game.

It was an unfair trade. I took the deal. It was a steal of a deal. It was the trade of a lifetime. Actually it was the deal of all eternity. I got everything and He got the short end of the stick.

I got peace with God. He became my Father and I became His child. I got a home in Heaven for eternity. I got help for each day and the Comforter residing in me. I got promises and guarantees that I will never be alone. I will never be forsaken. I got hope for today and for tomorrow. I got forgiveness. What did He get?

I look down at my hands. My hands are empty. I have nothing to give Him. Nothing! What did this trade cost Him?

As I read Psalm 22 I am reminded of the price He paid. I am reminded of the unfair deal. I know the trade He made.

Psalm 22:1 "My God, my God, why hast thou forsaken me?..."

He got loneliness and separation from His Father.

Psalm 22:13 "They gaped upon me with their mouths, as a ravening and a roaring lion."

He got mockery and disdain. He got humiliation.

Psalm 22:14 "I am poured out like water, and all my bones are out of joint: my heart is like wax; it is melted in the midst of my bowels."

He got pain and agony.

Psalm 22:15 "My strength is dried up like a potsherd; and my tongue cleaveth to my jaws; and thou hast brought me into the dust of death."

He got thirst and dryness.

Psalm 22:16 "For dogs have compassed me: the assembly of the wicked have inclosed me: they pierced my hands and my feet."

He got a cruel death.

I look down at my hands again. They are still empty, yet I realize they are covered in blood. I have nothing of value to trade and I am guilty! He pressed forward with the deal anyway. He interceded with His blood for me. He knew the true value and still made the trade. My sins were placed upon Him.

To some it was nothing more than a game. They "tossed the dice" at the foot of His cross.

Psalm 22:18 "They part my garments among them, and cast lots upon my vesture."

I looked down at my hands and saw the dice. The dice were smeared in blood from my guilty hands; I tossed them from me. It is no game. I did not want to play that game. So, I bowed my knees and took the deal. His life for mine.

Day 58
That Is It! I've Had Enough! (Psalm 23:1)

This weekend was tough. Talk about feeling inadequate! The day before church day, my husband told me that I would not have a translator for children's class. Stress washed over me like a raging river. I had my class all prepared and planned out based on having a translator. "I cannot do this!"

I seem to feel that way a lot. "I cannot do this!" Sometimes as a mom I feel the weight and magnitude of the responsibility of parenting. Some days I feel helpless and insufficient. Some days I question what I am doing. Some days I have a meltdown. I feel like a loser mom. "I cannot do this!"

I remember when we moved to our new country. It took a few months, but culture shock descended like a cloud. Once it did, I was overwhelmed. I remember standing at the sink washing dishes in freezing water, feeling chilled to the bone because we do not have a heated home, and feeling isolated because of language barrier. I broke down in tears. "I cannot do this!"

You know what God did? He did not say, "Yes, you can. You are amazing and gifted!" Nor did He say, "Hang in there and have some determination!"

When I said, "I cannot do this," God said, "No, no you cannot, but I can."

Psalm 23:1 "The LORD is my shepherd; I shall not want."

I shall not want. It means I shall lack nothing. It is easy to apply this to physical provision, but it goes beyond that. Yes, God supplies food, shelter, clothes, and other physical needs, but our Shepherd supplies so much more.

I cannot parent these kids! And God says, "No, no you cannot, but I can. Follow me."

I cannot teach this class! "No, no you cannot, but I can. Follow my lead."

I cannot live here! I cannot reach these people! I cannot play the piano or minister to the ladies or learn this language! No, I cannot, but He can through me if I follow His lead. He is my Shepherd, and anywhere He leads He will also provide what is needed.

It is easy to believe "the LORD is my shepherd; I shall not want" when it comes to our daily physical needs, but what about the needs we have to accomplish what He has called us to do?

- How can I parent these children? Follow the Shepherd.
- How can I teach this children's class? Follow the Shepherd.
- How can I _____? Follow the Shepherd. You will not lack anything!

1 Thessalonians 5:24 "Faithful is he that calleth you, who also will do it."

Day 59
The Funnel of Love (Psalm 23:1)

My son moved back to the States in July. That left his bedroom available to create a guestroom. I have never had a guestroom before, so this was pretty exciting. We host a lot of people in our home throughout the year including nationals, foreigners, and visiting pastors. Having a room dedicated to housing them is perfect.

We cleaned out my son's room. That was no small task! I bet I found three pounds of popcorn kernels. I organized the wardrobe with bedding, towels, and washcloths. Then on top of the wardrobe was a collection of blankets that needed to be organized. Since we house a lot of people, and since our house is not heated in the winter, we had accumulated many blankets. Oh! how pleasant it is to see God's provision!

Psalm 23:1 "The LORD is my shepherd; I shall not want."

I shall not want! I will not lack anything. The blessings of God were overflowing in our home in the form of blankets.

A few weeks later, I was speaking with someone. I knew it would be their first winter here, so I just bluntly asked if they were ready for it. They were not. They were in need of blankets. As I thought about our abundance of blankets at home, I realized that I had "built bigger barns."

Imagine a farmer. It is harvest season, and he has an amazing crop ready to be harvested. It is more than he needs this year and next year, and it is even too much for his barns to store. What does he do? Does he build bigger barns and hoard it all for him and his family, or does he choose to be a funnel for the Lord? A funnel passes on the blessings.

Here we were with our abundance of blankets. We have so many blankets that we have blankets downstairs just so we do not have to walk upstairs to get our other blankets. We have blankets for warmer months and blankets for colder months. We have blankets of different colors in case I want to change the color of the bedding to make it more decorative. I had a choice: bigger barns or be a funnel of love.

1 John 3:17 "But whoso hath this world's good, and seeth his brother have need, and shutteth up his bowels of compassion from him, how dwelleth the love of God in him?"

The Shepherd's provision is amazing and abundant. We are blessed! There is no shame in that. That is something to be celebrated. I shall not want! God is really good to us, but how tightly do we cling to those blessings? It is good to plan for the future and to be prepared, but when we trust in our barns full of goods instead of trusting in God's provision we are doing wrong. Sometimes God blesses us abundantly so that we can minister to the needs of others.

The Lord really is my Shepherd and I shall not want. Neither shall I hoard and close up my bowels of compassion.

Day 60
The Rest of the Story (Psalm 23:2)

If you were to be able to be a fly on the wall in my home, one thing you would notice is that from the moment I get up I am a flurry of activity. I think I resemble an out-of-control pinball zipping back and forth. I got that from my Dad, I think. He was very much the same way. The best way to describe us is fireballs of energy always on the go. By the time lunch rolls around, I usually have checked off dozens of items on my to-do list.

- Get up
- Make bed
- Get dressed
- Do devotion and prayer
- Check emails/Facebook
- Run 5K
- Make breakfast and eat
- Get kids started in school
- Dust house
- Sweep house
- Vacuum bedrooms
- Wipe down bathrooms
- Clean window sills
- Sweep porches
- Run to the store
- Make lunch
- Eat

That is just my average Monday before lunch to-do list. Like I said, flurry of activity. The after-lunch list is just as crazy. The most difficult thing for me is to be forced to sit and do nothing. Last year when I had to have my pacemaker installed (yes, I have a pacemaker at age 40!) the first thing I asked the doctor was not "How dangerous is this surgery?" or "How long will I be in the hospital?" My question was, "When can I start running again?"

Here is a problem, though. We have a tendency to equate this flurry of activity and long to-do lists with spirituality. God puts a high value on learning to rest.

Psalm 23:2 "He maketh me to lie down in green pastures..."

Sometimes to get me to rest, God has to make me lie down. When I had the pacemaker put in and when I had my gall bladder removed are good examples. Sometimes I struggle to hear His voice when He says, "Go lie down." I am more like Martha than Mary. I am Martha on overdrive. I do not usually complain about not having help. I enjoy the work, but sometimes I forget God wants me to stop and rest at His feet. Why?

I have to admit that sometimes my truck load of a to-do list is a source of pride. I am a highly productive person, and it makes me feel spiritual, important, and useful. I equate productivity with spirituality. When my husband asks me how my day was, my day is judged on how productive I was. If my to-do list was accomplished I smile big and say, "It was productive!"

Yet Jesus praised Mary's choice to sit at His feet. He did not have to force Mary to sit still. She chose to lie down in green pastures.

Luke 10:42 "But one thing is needful: and
Mary hath chosen that good part, which
shall not be taken away from her."

Me? He seems to repeatedly have to physically make me lie down. I am that crazy sheep in the pasture running around sweeping up leaves, inventorying the blades of grass, bopping from sheep to sheep asking how their meal is, checking the sun in the sky to see what time it is, and preparing for when it is time to move again. All the while, the Shepherd, in His kindness and wisdom, is saying, "Rest!"

Matthew 11:28-30 "Come unto me, all ye
that labour and are heavy laden, and I
will give you rest. Take my yoke upon
you, and learn of me; for I am meek and
lowly in heart: and ye shall find rest unto
your souls. For my yoke is easy, and my
burden is light."

Do not equate productivity with spirituality. Spirituality is following the Shepherd's lead. When He says work, it is time to work. When He says rest, lie down!

Day 61
Ordering at the Drive Thru Window
(Psalm 23:2)

There is something I miss more than I thought I would. When we moved here, we knew life would be very different than in the States. There are some aspects of life in the States that we did not realize are a large part of our culture and habits until we did not have access to those things.

I miss drive-thru windows. (I know. Silly to miss that, eh?)

As a mom, no matter what country I live in at the time, I am busy. In the States when I was busy running errands, it was nice to drive up to a fast food window and order something. I really liked the pharmacy drive-thru window. When you have a sick kid with you it sure is handy not to have to get out of the car. But here?

The closest I have to a drive-thru window is my fruit lady's little roadside shop. I can pull over to the side of the road and call out, "Can you grab me a dozen bananas?" She is kind enough to save me from having to get out of the car or off the scooter, and she delivers the bananas three whole steps across the sidewalk. I love my fruit lady drive-thru "window."

Psalm 23:2 "He maketh me to lie down in green pastures: he leadeth me beside the still waters."

The fact is, we cannot always lie down in green pastures. There are times when we need to stop everything and rest, but the majority of the time we must be busy about the Father's business.

How can we find rest and peace when we are always on the go? We have dishes to wash, mouths to feed, floors to sweep, shopping, and teaching Sunday school. It is not like there is a drive-thru window where we can pull up and order rest and peace to go. Or is there?

Actually, there is! Sometimes we lie down "in green pastures" and find rest and peace. Other times we are on the go beside the still waters," and we can still find rest and peace. The key is following where He leads.

There is rest and peace when we follow His lead. Our problem is that we get ahead of Him, or we veer off on a path He is not leading us down. When we stay right there with Him, letting Him lead, we can rest peacefully knowing that no matter what the terrain looks like around us, those still waters are right there. He will take care of us.

Do you feel like the waters are raging around you? Instead of still waters do you hear the gushing of whitewater rapids? Do you have the busy, on-the-go life and you struggle to find the still waters as you go? Check to see how closely you are following the Shepherd's lead.

It may be that you are trying to lead. It may be that you have veered down the wrong path. It may also be that you have forgotten to roll down your window and order a Rest Combo Meal, Biggy Sized with a side order of Peace from the Still Waters drive-thru window. It is there for the asking if you are following His lead and trusting Him. He leadeth me beside the still waters, am I following?

Day 62
Roof Repair (Psalm 23:2-4)

Years ago when we lived in the States, we owned a house. It was an old home that took a lot of work to get it looking nice. We added a master bedroom suite, remodeled the kitchen and main bathroom, added a deck, changed the siding, and more.

One day a violent storm came through the area. There was thunder and lightning. There was also hail-- very large hail. It pounded our roof and damaged the shingles. When the storm was finished, my husband knew we better act fast in getting the shingles replaced. If it rained, there was a possibility of water damage from a leaky roof. We called the insurance company, and then we called a roofing company. The roof was replaced, and our house was ready for the next storm.

A few years ago, our family faced a different type of storm. Its impact was intense. We endured a major earthquake of 7.8 magnitude. Our family experienced months of rescue and recovery efforts. The physical, emotional, and spiritual strain began to take its toll on our family. We were drained. We needed to be restored desperately. It was at that point we chose to take a time away from ministry for a couple of weeks.

We knew that if we faced another storm at that moment, we would not be ready. The potential for serious damage was greatly increased in our weakness. Just like when we took the time to replace the roof on our house years before, we took the time for repairing ourselves and our family. Just like we could not replace our roof on our house ourselves (we had to call a roofing company), we also could not repair the damage done during the storm of the earthquake. We had to call out for help.

Storms in life can drain us physically, emotionally, and spiritually.

The Lord refreshes us physically.
He knows when we need physical rest.

> *Psalm 23:2 "He maketh me to lie down in green pastures: he leadeth me beside the still waters."*

The Lord restores us emotionally.
Storms in life can leave us emotionally drained, raw, or even numb. He knows how to heal it.

> *Psalm 23:3 "He restoreth my soul..."*

The Lord revitalizes us spiritually.
He can get us back on the right path when spiritually we become weary in well doing during a storm.

> *Psalm 23:3 "... he leadeth me in the paths of righteousness for his name's sake."*

Why is it so important to make sure these areas are well maintained? Why do we need to take the time to inspect the damage from storms? Why do we need to take it seriously? Because the next storm may be just around the corner.

Psalm 23:4 "Yea, though I walk through the valley of the shadow of death, I will fear no evil: for thou art with me; thy rod and thy staff they comfort me."

The fact is that there are storms in life. How do we get through them? How do we survive? In our own strength? That would be like my husband and I climbing on the roof of our home and replacing the roof ourselves. I can promise you that if we replaced a roof, when the next storm came the house would be a disaster! No, the only way to survive storms is to call in the Professional. He prepares us for the storms of life and then leads us through those storms of life. (I will fear no evil: for thou art with me!)

As you go through storms, pay attention to the condition of your "roof." If you are physically, emotionally, or spiritually drained, go to the One who restores. Do not delay. Get alone with Him. Take time to be refreshed, restored, and revitalized. Prepare for the next storm. When that storm comes, do not fear. He is with you.

Day 63
That is Mine! (Psalm 24:1)

There is an adorable little girl in our church. We love her so much. She is around four years old, and she is the cutest little thing you have ever seen. There is a small problem, though. She is undisciplined, so she can get into trouble quicker than you can catch her to stop her.

One of the nasty habits she has picked up is rummaging through other people's bags at church. We guard our pocket books closely because if we do not we will find her wandering around the church carrying our sunglasses, water bottles, or wallets.

I have chosen to use the opportunity to teach her authority and respect for the property of others. When she goes to reach in my bag, with a firm but loving voice I say, "Dina, no. That is mine." Inevitably, she reaches in the bag again every time. I grab her hand, firmly push it away, and again say, "Dina, no. That is not yours. That is mine." Sometimes I will bring things to share with her. I will wait until she is looking and then I will reach in my bag. I grab the toy and give it to her. "Dina, here. Take this. You may play with this."

Sometimes she gets a pen from someone's bag. As I am sitting in church, I turn to see the young girl wielding the mighty object of destruction. With a songbook as her coloring book, the young child happily makes her mark in the world. I jump up and take the pen and book from her. "No, Dina. That is not good." She must learn to take care of other people's things. She is learning, but it will take time. She is worth the effort.

Psalm 24:1 "The earth is the LORD'S, and
the fulness thereof; the world, and they
that dwell therein."

I am sometimes just like Dina more than I realize. Everything in the earth is the Lord's. It all belongs to Him. Sometimes I want to take things that are His, and He says, "No." I get upset and keep trying because I really want it. He continues to push my hand away and says, "No. That is mine and you may not have it."

Honestly, I really would love a dishwasher, endless supply of cheddar cheese, Krispy Kreme donuts, and vehicles that never break down. I would love my oldest child sitting at the Thanksgiving table, and to hear my Dad's voice once more. Those things belong to God. He has chosen to say, "No, you may not have it." Do I keep grabbing at those things like Dina grabbing in my bag?

Sometimes He lets me have some things to "play" with. They are still His, though. Sometimes He finds me destroying His property and not taking care of it like I should. I think of my time. It is actually His time because I belong to Him. Sometimes I waste time. Much like Dina coloring in the hymnal, I abuse His property of time.

I think of my husband and children. They really do not belong to me. They belong to Him. Am I treating them with the respect I should? I would never color in the church hymnals, but do I scribble on the hearts of my family with my words?

I think of the home where He has allowed me to live. Am I taking care of it? Am I using it for His glory?

I think of the ministry. It is not my ministry. It is His. Do I give my best? Do I do damage to His ministry with my actions?

The "fulness" of the earth is His. That means whatever is in the earth belongs to Him. Do I respect His property? Do I take without permission? Do I damage His property?

Just as I think Dina is worth the time and effort to train, God also thinks that of me. I want to be teachable.

Day 64
Know-It-All Christianity (Psalm 25)

My youngest child is an adventure every day. He is fun, unique, and a lot like his Dad and Grampa. He has many traits that I love, but there is one trait about him that is my favorite. He is teachable.

The boy is a sponge! He loves to learn new things. Right now he is learning piano from his piano teacher. He is learning how to be a better artist from his sister. He is learning about tools, bicycle repair, cars, and machinery from his Dad. From me, he is learning how to cook, how to be a better writer, and how to make good outlines. His heart's desire is to be a pastor one day, so learning to make good outlines would be a handy skill.

Psalm 25:4 "Shew me thy ways, O LORD;
teach me thy paths."

When I read Psalm 25, I was amazed at how many times it mentions the word "teach". That word is used five times. The word "shew" is used twice, and the words "lead" and "guide" are each used once. One of David's greatest traits was that he was teachable. What makes a person teachable?

- A desire to see- "Shew me thy ways..." (vs 4)
- A willingness to follow- "Lead me..." (vs 5)
- A hunger for truth- "Lead me in thy truth..." (vs 5)
- Patience- "... on thee do I wait all the day." (vs 5)

- Humility- "The meek will he guide..." (vs 9)
- Respect for the Teacher- "What man is he that feareth the LORD? him shall he teach..." (vs 12)

Our God is a willing Teacher, because He is good and upright.

> Psalm 25:8 "Good and upright is the LORD: therefore will he teach sinners in the way."

I love when my son comes in the kitchen and asks if he can help. What he is really saying is, "I want to learn how to do that, Mom." It thrills my heart to take those moments and work with him. It brings great joy to a teacher when a student has such a willingness to learn. God is the same way with us. He greatly delights in teaching us. He loves when we crawl up in His lap and say, "Teach me."

On the flip side, there is nothing more frustrating to a teacher than to try to help someone by teaching them when they are convinced they know everything they need to know. As a teacher, it literally pains me to watch someone struggle unnecessarily when they could simply humble themselves and admit they do not have all the answers.

I wonder how God sees me when I refuse to look to Him and learn instead of struggling on my own path with my own plans, ideas, and logic. Know-It-All Christianity is a painful road.

How teachable are we? Are we hungry sponges, soaking up all that we can as He teaches?

Or are we convinced we already have all the answers?

> *Psalm 25:5 "Lead me in thy truth, and teach me: for thou art the God of my salvation; on thee do I wait all the day."*

Day 65
Video Game Disaster (Psalm 26)

Several years ago, our family had a video game we enjoyed playing together. I am not much of a video game person, but I really enjoyed that one because it was a simple game we could all play together. In the game, each player had armed vehicles and a home base. The goal was to take your armed vehicles and destroy your opponent's home base while still protecting your own base. If the enemy was attacking your home base, a computer voice would announce, "Base under attack." That would warn you to go back and fight the enemy to get them off your territory. Your home base would have battle scars, soot, and sometimes a small fire.

As the game progressed, if your home base sustained significant damage, the computer would give you a countdown. "Structural integrity 30%." I loved the warnings because sometimes I get tunnel vision. If I was busily attacking vehicles or the opponent's home base, sometimes I would forget to protect my own base. When the warnings came, I knew to change my priorities: protect the home base.

If the attack continued, the announcement would come, "Structural integrity 15%... Structural integrity 5%... Structural integrity failing." If the attack was not stopped my home base was destroyed, and I would lose the game. (I hate to lose!)

Integrity: Completeness, innocence (in the Bible, moral innocence.)

In a video game, integrity means that the base was unharmed and undefiled. It was complete, strong, and in great shape. In life, it means we are not defiled. We stand in moral innocence, strong and clean.

> *Psalm 26:1 "Judge me, O LORD; for I have walked in mine integrity: I have trusted also in the LORD; therefore I shall not slide."*

David was declaring that his home base (self) was at 100% structural integrity. His spiritual integrity had not been marred or defiled. He was guarding his integrity and did not want to give any part of it away. He knew that if he guarded his spiritual integrity and kept it at 100%, he would never hear the countdown slide, "Spiritual integrity 30%... Spiritual integrity 15%... Spiritual integrity failing..."

How did he guard his integrity? He did not let the enemy hang out at his home base!

> *Psalm 26:4-5 "I have not sat with vain persons, neither will I go in with dissemblers. I have hated the congregation of evil doers; and will not sit with the wicked."*

He did not hang out with corrupt people, people with wicked agendas, time wasters, and people who were morally defiled. Separation was a big deal to David. It is also a big deal to our God.

> *James 4:4 "Ye adulterers and adulteresses, know ye not that the friendship of the world is enmity with God? whosoever therefore will be a friend of the world is the enemy of God."*

We do not reach the world for Christ by being like the world. We do not have intimate fellowship with ungodly people. We do not seek their counsel. We do not embrace their close friendship.

Does that mean we just sit at our home base to keep ungodly people off? No. We go out and reach the world with the Gospel. We love them and reach out to them. Our desire is to be used by the Lord to help destroy the hold that sin has on them by sharing the truth about salvation with them. Separation should never become isolation, but we should heed the warnings from God's Word and from His Spirit when our home base is under attack.

> *Psalm 26:11 "But as for me, I will walk in mine integrity: redeem me, and be merciful unto me."*

Guard your home base.

Day 66
Heart's Desire (Psalm 27:4)

I love conversation-starter questions. I have a jar that I use with my children when we have private snack time. The jar contains slips of paper with simple questions on them to help us grow in our fellowship and keep our lines of communication open. We take turns drawing a piece of paper out and reading it. Then we both answer the question. Some of the questions:

- "What makes you laugh?"
- "What makes you sad?"
- "If you could go anywhere in the world, where would you go?"
- "If you could meet anyone in history, who would you meet?"

There are twenty questions in the jar. That jar has helped us have amazing times of fellowship. In Psalm 27, it is almost like someone asked David a conversation-starter question. "David, if you could only have one thing, what would it be?"

Psalm 27:4 "One thing have I desired of the LORD, that will I seek after; that I may dwell in the house of the LORD all the days of my life, to behold the beauty of the LORD, and to enquire in his temple."

Of all the things David could have said...

- That my enemies would be destroyed.
- That I would have a vast empire.
- That I would never grow old.
- That I could bathe in chocolate fountains twice a day. (That be a dream indeed!)

David said, "If I could just have one thing it would be to dwell in the place where God meets with His people." He longed for constant, close intimacy with God. He did not want to just have a temple. He did not want just to visit the temple. He wanted to dwell in the house of the Lord. He hungered for God. There was nothing in the world that held his heart the way his God did. He would willingly set everything else in life aside for the Lord. It was his love and his pursuit.

Where is my heart? If I could only have one thing, what would it be? Would it be material things like a house, land, or wealth? Would I long for beauty, power, or fame? Would I choose family or friends? Would I long for health and long life? Would I ask for safety for my family? Would success be my heart's desire? If I could only have one thing, would I choose, without hesitation and with honest desire and longing, to live out the rest of my days in intense, close, intimate fellowship with my Saviour, Jesus?

I'd rather have Jesus than silver or gold;
I'd rather be His than have riches untold;
I'd rather have Jesus than houses or lands;
I'd rather be led by His nail-pierced hand.

Refrain:
Than to be the king of a vast domain
Or be held in sin's dread sway;
I'd rather have Jesus than anything
This world affords today.

I'd rather have Jesus than men's applause;
I'd rather be faithful to His dear cause;
I'd rather have Jesus than worldwide fame;
I'd rather be true to His holy name.

He is fairer than lilies of rarest bloom;
He is sweeter than honey from out the comb;
He is all that my hungering spirit needs;
I'd rather have Jesus and let Him lead.

Day 67
It is a Match (Psalm 28:3)

Last night, my husband and I spent a few minutes with the kids playing one of our favorite games. We all sat down in the living room floor and played UNO. We dealt the cards and began playing. The game is pretty simple to play so it works for a wide range of ages. One just has to match either the color or the number of a card to play it on the discard pile.

When we play, sometimes it goes pretty fast. Someone will play a green number two. The next person will play a green number five. The next person will play a red number five. If the following person is not paying attention, in their haste they will try to play a green card, like a green number seven. The problem is that the color has been changed to red. The card does not match. We all get a good laugh and the person has to pick their green card back up.

Do you play green sevens to cover up red fives?

Psalm 28:3 "Draw me not away with the wicked, and with the workers of iniquity, which speak peace to their neighbours, but mischief is in their hearts."

David said one of the characteristics of a wicked person is that their words do not match their hearts. They say kind things to their neighbor's face, but in their hearts they have a secret and selfish agenda. They have wicked motives. They are workers of iniquity. They cover their wicked "red five" heart with pleasant "green seven" words.

Is that how we want to be? Do we want to imitate the character of workers of iniquity? The solution is to let your words match your heart and your heart match your words. Let it all match the mind and heart of Christ. Be real. Be genuine. Do not speak kindly to someone while harboring ill will, bad feelings, or selfish motives toward them. In God's UNO game, He does not want you to take up the green number seven. He wants you to get rid of the red number five you are trying to cover up.

Day 68
The Soldier and the Bride (Psalm 29:1-2)

I come from a family of military people. My Dad was in the Army for eight years. My uncle was career military in the Army. I have several cousins and uncles who are serving or have served in the military. One thing I must say, whether in pictures or in person, there is something powerful about seeing them in uniform. It commands respect. That uniform symbolizes so much. When you see them in uniform, you know that person has given their best. They are in top physical condition. They have been trained. They are soldiers, and yet there is Someone greater who deserves these fine-looking men and women in their finest military attire to bow their knees.

> Psalm 29:1 "Give unto the LORD, O ye
> mighty, give unto the LORD glory and
> strength."

Mighty, strong, and glorious as they may be, their victories and their accomplishments are only due to the might, grace, and strength of the Lord. Our most physically elite and battle-prepared representatives on earth cannot compare to the strength and might of the Lord. Their honor and glory should go to Him.

How beautiful to see these soldiers-- these warriors-- bow their knees and give glory where it is truly due! If that be the case, how much more should I, weak and pitiful as I am, give God glory for all victories?

Elegant. Pure. Glowing. Clean. Beautiful. She walks down the aisle and the congregation rises to their feet. Her pure white dress shines. She is breathtaking. The virgin bride reaches the front of the sanctuary to meet her groom. The vows are said, and then it happens. The first kiss they have ever experienced. They saved it for each other.

It is a stunning picture of the beauty of holiness. She saved herself for him. She was set apart for him and him alone. Radiant beauty. It captivates the whole audience, and yet there is Someone's holiness that it more pure and more beautiful. He deserves the glory, the honor, and the praise.

Psalm 29:2 "Give unto the LORD the glory due unto his name; worship the LORD in the beauty of holiness."

A pure virgin bride in her cleanest, whitest, most perfect gown, even she should bow the knee and give glory where it is truly due. He is holy, and His holiness is absolutely pure, clean, perfect, sinless, and set apart. It is beautiful. Oh, to see such a pure and beautiful bride in her gown bow the knee to the One who deserves the glory! How much more does He deserve all the glory from someone like me!

Weak, stained with sin, hopeless, helpless. How could I ever take the glory for victories? I am no soldier. I am no radiant bride in a pure white gown. What a tragedy, what an insult if I boast in accomplishments! Give unto the Lord glory and worship Him in the beauty of holiness. He is the only one truly worthy.

Day 69
The Voice (Psalm 29)

Have you ever been in a trial and felt like you could not hear His voice? Were you calling out to Him, yet you felt so alone? Maybe you are dealing with a trial like that right now. Psalm 29 explains a few things about God by using the description of His voice.

God is with us through the trial no matter what the trial is. No matter how high, how wide, or how deep the trial is, He is bigger. He is with us through the storm and He is with us through the deep waters.

Psalm 29:3 "The voice of the LORD is upon the waters: the God of glory thundereth: the LORD is upon many waters."

Even in the trial He is still in control, sitting on His throne.

Psalm 29:4 "The voice of the LORD is powerful; the voice of the LORD is full of majesty."

He is greater than the dark forests of trials, and He can easily remove the obstacles that are too big for us.

Psalm 29:5 "The voice of the LORD breaketh the cedars; yea, the LORD breaketh the cedars of Lebanon."

Psalm 29:9 "The voice of the LORD maketh the hinds to calve, and discovereth the forests: and in his temple doth every one speak of his glory."

He is Lord over the fire and the flames that threaten to consume us.

Psalm 29:7 "The voice of the LORD divideth the flames of fire."

He is sovereign over the floods of life that try to sweep us away.

Psalm 29:10 "The LORD sitteth upon the flood; yea, the LORD sitteth King for ever."

He masters all these types of trials with ease, simply by the power of His voice. His booming, loud, bold voice. Yes, He is master over our trials and controls them at will, and yet our greatest need is not for His booming, powerful voice to remove the trial. That is the voice we often crave to hear, but the one we often need to hear most is different. It is easy to hear the big booming voice. We wait for it. We cry for it.

"Lord, take this trial away! It hurts!" We listen for His booming voice, and we cannot hear it.

It is in those moments we can learn how to listen for His other voice. His still small voice. It is not the voice that removes trials, knocks down obstacles, and diverts the floods. It is the voice that speaks peace to our hears. You have to be quiet, still, and patient to hear it. His still... small... voice. It says, "I am here. I've got you. Peace."

1 Kings 19:11-12 "And he said, Go forth, and stand upon the mount before the LORD. And, behold, the LORD passed by, and a great and strong wind rent the mountains, and brake in pieces the rocks before the LORD; but the LORD was not in the wind: and after the wind an earthquake; but the LORD was not in the earthquake: And after the earthquake a fire; but the LORD was not in the fire: and after the fire a still small voice."

Day 70
Daddy's Girl (Psalm 30)

I am unapologetically a Daddy's girl. My Daddy has been in Heaven for almost six years now, and I still consider myself a Daddy's girl. I loved making him proud of me. I loved spending time with him. I loved watching football while eating cheese with him.

One thing I hated, though, was any time I disappointed him. I hated having to be disciplined. I did not just hate discipline because it was uncomfortable. I hated it because I knew my Daddy was not happy with what I had done. He still loved me. I never doubted that, but I treasured being in his favor. It was my heart's longing to stay in his favor.

I also loved the fact that I knew my Dad enough to know what would disappoint him. I knew he loved diligence and honesty. I knew he valued hard work and integrity. If I wanted his approval and to please him, those were character traits I had to have.

Psalm 30:4-5 "Sing unto the LORD, O ye saints of his, and give thanks at the remembrance of his holiness. For his anger endureth but a moment; in his favour is life: weeping may endure for a night, but joy cometh in the morning."

Favor- approval, support, or liking for someone or something. To delight in. To go beyond what is due or usual.

I love dwelling on the holiness of God. It is consistent and dependable. He never changes. It is easy to respect and adore our God who displays the beauty of holiness and purity. Because of His holiness, I know sin will disappoint Him. I know it will bring His chastisement. Just as my earthly Dad chastised me when I did wrong, my Heavenly Father does the same. He loves me and wants to teach me.

The times of chastisement are never pleasant, but I know He has a purpose rooted in love. Not only that, but His chastisement will not be forever. He is not doing it to destroy me. He is doing it to train me and to bring me back into His favor. Oh, how I treasure being in His favor! It is life!

His favor is not what I deserve. His favor is beyond what is due. It is overwhelming, sweet, good, and precious! Yes, His discipline teaches me to do right, but it is His favor that makes me hunger to follow Him.

Give thanks when you recall the holiness of God. It is pure and perfect. It brings His chastisement upon us when we stray. Treasure His favor, because in His favor is life. Let His favor draw you to repentance. The goodness of God leads to repentance. If you are being chastised, remember that it is not going to last forever. Humble yourself and submit to His loving chastisement. Joy comes in the morning.

Day 71
Lying Vanities (Psalm 31)

It is an unpleasant part of the life I live. I am surrounded by it. It is inescapable. I can look out my windows and see it. I walk down the street and see it. It is in the stores. It is on vehicles. It is everywhere.

Idolatry surrounds me. Yesterday we came home from church. I looked out my kitchen window to see my neighbors doing worship with their priest. They were chanting and making offerings to idols. The conch horn was blown several times. Incense was burning all around them. Statues in the yard were decorated.

On the way to and from church I noticed a tree wrapped in worship garland and a large stone colored in worship powders. Many people had the red worship dot on their foreheads, and the temples were teaming with people. My heart breaks, but then I wonder: am I also guilty?

Psalm 31:6 "I have hated them that regard lying vanities: but I trust in the LORD."

Lying vanity- deceiving emptiness

What is a lying vanity? Is it statues that cannot hear or see? Is it trees that cannot help? Is it chants and incense and red dots on foreheads? Those things surely are lying vanities, but this term covers much more. The verse gives a perfect definition. David gave a comparison here that makes it clear exactly what a lying vanity is. He said that he has hated those who regard lying vanities, but then he explained the opposite of lying vanities. He trusted in the Lord. A lying vanity is anything that is not trusting the Lord. It is more than just physical idols or pagan worship.

Am I guilty? Every time I trust in something other than the Lord, yes, I am guilty! When I trust in my own strength, I am guilty. When I trust in my wisdom and logic, I am guilty. When I trust in people or government or education or finances...

Deceptive. These things look so trustworthy. They look like they will solve our problems. They look like the answers, yet they are emptiness.

The opposite is to trust in the Lord. He is the answer to our needs and our problems. He is the solution.

What are we trusting? Are we regarding lying vanities? Do we pridefully think that our lying vanities are better than those of people who bow down to statues and trees?

Day 72
Hide and Seek (Psalm 32)

I love playing Hide-and-Seek with young children. There is nothing more humorous than when they find what they think is the perfect hiding place, and yet they are easily seen. Many children think if they cannot see you, then surely you cannot see them. They cover themselves with a blanket in the middle of the floor and are convinced you will not suspect that the huge, wiggling lump is really them hiding. They giggle and wiggle in their hiding spot and are totally surprised when you uncover them and begin a tickle war.

We also play Hide-and-Seek much the same way, but our game is not so funny. We attempt to cover our sin as if God cannot see the big pile in the center of our hearts. He is not giggling and laughing. There is nothing funny about our game. Our game is more like the child who stole the cake. Smudges of chocolate all over his face, and the child insists he did not eat the cake. He is completely perplexed how anyone could know he consumed the stolen delight.

Smudges of sin all over our hands and hearts, we try to hide our transgression. We are filled with guile, trickery, deceit, falsehood. We think our hidden sin will bring us happiness. As long as no one finds out, we will be happy. David declared quite the opposite.

Psalm 32:1 "Blessed is he whose transgression is forgiven, whose sin is

covered. Blessed is the man unto whom
the LORD imputeth not iniquity, and in
whose spirit there is no guile."

David declares happiness is not in hidden sin, but in forgiven sin, covered not by us but by His blood and cleansed. Happiness is not in deceit and trickery (guile), but it is found in a right relationship with the Lord. Happiness is not in hiding. Instead, it is in seeking.

Psalm 32:3-4 "When I kept silence, my
bones waxed old through my roaring all
the day long. For day and night thy hand
was heavy upon me: my moisture is
turned into the drought of summer.
Selah."

David explained what it was like to try to hide sin. He kept silence, and the conviction was a weight upon him. He lost joy and peace. The refreshing babbling brook of joy dried up to dust, but when he confessed his sin and repented, things changed.

Psalm 32:5 "I acknowledged my sin unto
thee, and mine iniquity have I not hid. I
said, I will confess my transgressions
unto the LORD; and thou forgavest the
iniquity of my sin. Selah."

Sweet peace and joy returned. The close fellowship with his God was restored. David then gave a warning as well.

Psalm 32:6 "For this shall every one that is godly pray unto thee in a time when thou mayest be found: surely in the floods of great waters they shall not come nigh unto him."

Godly people will call out for forgiveness because they understand two things:

1. **God may not always be found.** He convicts and deals with us, but if we continually reject and ignore Him, the consequences become more serious. Chastisement becomes more severe. For the lost person, God may stop dealing with them altogether. David says to seek the Lord when He is dealing with us.
2. **There is safety in a right relationship with the Lord.** We have heard it said many times, "The safest place on earth is in the center of God's will." It is true. David said that when we have a right relationship with the Lord, the floods of trials and tribulation cannot drown us and overtake us.

Are we harboring sin and hiding it? Are we covering it thinking there is joy as long as we are not caught? The real joy is found in repentance, confession, and having sin forgiven.

Day 73
Enduring to the End (Psalm 33:1-3)

Have you ever noticed people's faces as they sing in church? It is a little easier for me because I play the piano. Sometimes I glance down at the congregation. Some people look like they are in pain, enduring to the end of the song. Some people look cheerful and vibrant. Some people look like they are captivated by the song. Some look like their minds are a million miles away.

Psalm 33 is a powerful "music ministry" psalm. It teaches the importance of music in our worship. It even teaches us the mode and method of our singing and music.

> *Psalm 33:1-3 "Rejoice in the LORD, O ye righteous: for praise is comely for the upright. Praise the LORD with harp: sing unto him with the psaltery and an instrument of ten strings. Sing unto him a new song; play skilfully with a loud noise."*

Rejoice- To celebrate with joy

Singing to the Lord should not be a painful event that we endure. It is a form of praise that our Lord greatly desires. It is also "comely" for the upright. That means it is appropriate, beautiful, and attractive. When it comes to the music part of the church service, do you endure, or do you joyfully pour your heart into it knowing it is a vital part of our worship?

Praise- to express approval, admiration, gratitude, and respect

Music and song can show our gratitude and respect to the Lord. The music service should not be about us. It is about Him. Does the music we choose and the songs we sing reflect our focus on Him? Does the music selected display our respect for the Lord? If the music and songs mimic the world's music, it does not show the respect our holy God deserves. If the lyrics are unbiblical, the song does not honor the Lord. If the song is focused on us and not Him, it is not praising Him. If we select our music ministry based on what we like and want instead of what shows honor, respect, and gratitude, then our music ministry is no longer praise to God. It becomes praise to ourselves. If the music feeds our flesh, it is definitely not music He is interested in hearing.

Sing- to make musical sound with the voice

Singing is not optional. It is commanded in the Bible. God loves it when we sing to Him and about Him. The amazing thing is that the Lord hears the music of the heart. It is not about how lovely we sing with our voice (though we should do our best), but it is about giving Him our whole hearts while expressing praise in singing worship. We should also not allow our singing and music to become routine and dull. Sing unto Him a new song. That is not talking about putting a stamp of approval on CCM, or any fleshly music, simply because it is new. It is however talking about being willing to learn (or write) new songs to keep things fresh and vibrant. Our singing should never be mere habit, even when we are singing songs that have been around for centuries.

Play- to operate a musical instrument

Playing musical instruments is a vital part of the music ministry and worship service. It is a worthy investment to spend our time learning to play an instrument and encouraging our children to learn an instrument. Notice, though, that it says to play *skilfully*. That takes time and effort. It takes practice. We should not "wing it" for the Lord. When those who play instruments put the time and effort into learning their instruments to the best of their ability, their playing becomes a beautiful offering on the altar of praise. When we treat our playing of instruments flippantly, it becomes little more than racket.

Remember, the Lord is looking at the heart. We do not have to be perfect concert pianists, but it does matter that we have put effort into learning our instruments the best that we can. We are worshiping the Creator of the universe. We need to give our very best and put the time into making our music worship one that honors and respects who He is.

The verse also says to play skilfully with a loud noise. When I sit down at the piano or psaltery, if I am playing a song I am still learning, I often play it timidly and quietly. When I have learned the song well, I play it confidently and loudly.

The music ministry and worship service matters. It matters also how we do it. Do it with joy.

Do it with respect, honor, gratitude, and admiration. Be involved: sing and play the instruments. Do it skilfully. He is worthy of us giving our very best at all times.

Day 74
Hot Tea Meditation (Psalm 33:4-8)

He did it again. Actually, he does it almost every morning. As I lie in the warmth of my bed early in the morning, my husband walks in carrying my hot tea. What a lovely way to wake up each day!

This morning it got me thinking about how blessed I am with such a wonderful husband. I began dwelling on his character and nature and how much I treasure who he is. The more I thought about who he is, the more my love for him swelled within my heart.

Then I sat down this morning to do my devotion. The Lord served up some "hot tea" from His Word. I read again today about how we should rejoice, praise, sing, and play instruments in honor and worship of God. (Psalm 33:1-3) Then I read the "why." Why should we rejoice, praise, sing, and play in worship of Him? Just as I meditated on the character and nature of my husband, I began meditating on the character and nature of my Father in Heaven.

Psalm 33:4-7 "For the word of the LORD is right; and all his works are done in truth. He loveth righteousness and judgment: the earth is full of the goodness of the LORD. By the word of the LORD were the heavens made; and all the host of them by the breath of his mouth. He gathereth the waters of the

sea together as an heap: he layeth up the
depth in storehouses."

Why does He deserve our praise and worship?

- Because His Word is right.
- Because His works are true.
- Because He is righteous
- Because He is just.
- Because He is good.
- Because He made us.
- Because He made everything!
- Because He is powerful.
- Because He is God.

Yes, we should worship and praise Him because these things are true, but if we take time to dwell on who God is, then worship and praise will bubble up out of us like a fountain. Sometimes we neglect simply thinking about who our God is. Sometimes our worship is shallow, dry, or nonexistent because we forget all He has done for us and all that He does for us each day. The more we dwell on His character and nature, the more our respect, reverence, love, and adoration for Him will swell into praise and worship.

Psalm 33:8 "Let all the earth fear the
LORD: let all the inhabitants of the world
stand in awe of him."

This verse is saying stop and think about who our God is. Stand in awe. He is worthy!

Day 75
Army Mom (Psalm 33:9-22)

And just like that...

I became an Army Mom. My oldest joined the military. I am not surprised. He has spoken about joining the military most of his life. He has almost always owned camouflage clothing of some sort-- desert camo, digital camo, etc.

He can tell you about every tank that has ever been used, what battles they were used in, and who would have used them. He can watch a military movie and pick out if the director used the right weaponry for the movie. More than once we have had to endure him yelling at the television about how that tank was not in that battle or that gun was not used during that time period. He would make an amazing military museum docent.

It is unmistakable that our family supports our military personnel. My Dad was a veteran of the Army. I have uncles and cousins who have served or are currently serving in the Army. My husband's Dad was a Navy man. Yes, military must be in my son's blood.

Our family has also been voters. We try to do our part as good citizens. We research candidates. We train our children how to seek God's will concerning voting. We teach them how to vote and always take them with us to the polls so that we can set the example. We pray for good leadership, and when the leader, good or bad, gets in office, we pray for them.

Psalm 33 gives a proper perspective of these two things. Though we are a patriotic family, our patriotism comes with limitations. It reminds us who our real Commander in Chief is. Though we show respect and honor to our government leaders, our ultimate loyalty must be with the King of kings and Lord of lords.

> Psalm 33:9 "For he spake, and it was done; he commanded, and it stood fast."

Everything and everyone is under His command and authority. In the military, when a commanding officer gives an order, that command must be followed. There is no choice in the matter. Think about our God's commands. His authority is not just over people. His authority stretches over all creation. He spoke the world and the heavens into existence. He has complete sovereignty.

Do we put our trust and confidence in government leaders? Are we looking to a president to solve our problems?

> Psalm 33:10 "The LORD bringeth the counsel of the heathen to nought: he maketh the devices of the people of none effect."

But our God's counsel?

Psalm 33:11 "The counsel of the LORD
standeth for ever, the thoughts of his
heart to all generations."

Psalm 33 gives a contrast between the two. God's Word is sure and permanent. His ways are perfect. That is why a nation that chooses to follow Him will be blessed.

Psalm 33:12 "Blessed is the nation whose
God is the LORD; and the people whom
he hath chosen for his own inheritance."

There is such a temptation to trust man's logic and wisdom, but man's logic and wisdom is faulty and temporary. There is also a temptation to trust in force, strength, and weaponry. I am a supporter of the Second Amendment. I love our freedom and right to bear arms. I love that we have a strong military. I even love that in a few weeks my son will be wearing an official Army uniform, but my trust is not in a conceal-and-carry weapon. It is not in my husband's aim and his readiness to defend our family. It is not in the power and might of our American military.

Psalm 33:17 "An horse is a vain thing for
safety: neither shall he deliver any by his
great strength."

Our weaponry is vanity. True power and safety comes from the One who sees all and commands all from His throne in Heaven. Yes, there is wisdom in being prepared. Yes, there is wisdom in a nation having a strong, well-trained military, but our trust should not be placed in the guns in our hands.

Instead, our confidence should be placed in the God on the throne.

> *Psalm 33:18-19 "Behold, the eye of the LORD is upon them that fear him, upon them that hope in his mercy; To deliver their soul from death, and to keep them alive in famine."*

I have been asked many times how I felt about my son going into the military. How do I feel?

Total peace. It is not because of the gun in his hand. It is not because of the armor around him. It is not because of leaders or government. My peace comes from knowing that my God is sitting on the throne of Heaven has His watchful eye over my son. Nothing can happen to him without God's permission.

> *Psalm 33:20-22 "Our soul waiteth for the LORD: he is our help and our shield. For our heart shall rejoice in him, because we have trusted in his holy name. Let thy mercy, O LORD, be upon us, according as we hope in thee."*

Day 76
Power Problems (Psalm 34)

It has been one of those mornings. Have you ever had one of those mornings where it seems like the harder you try to be a help, the more you mess things up? (Enter pity party.)

I got out of bed this morning with a flourish. I was ready to start my long list of things that needed to be done. I wanted to be a good help to my husband, so the first thing I did was I turned on the electric heater. I wanted him to have a warm room when he awoke. Then I rushed downstairs and turned on the iron to iron his clothes. I decided while the iron was heating up I would make his coffee. I put water in the electric kettle and turned it on.

I grabbed the slow cooker out of the fridge and put it on the counter. It had our lunch in it. I plugged it in to get it started. Then I realized my husband had coffee in his thermos I could heat in the microwave, so he could have one cup of coffee quickly. I poured the coffee in his favorite cup and pitched it into the microwave. I turned the microwave on, and suddenly power went out throughout the house. In my flurry of helpfulness, I did not realize how many electrical appliances I was using. I overloaded our electrical system. The husband I had been trying to help now had to spend time fixing the problem I made. I felt terrible.

While my husband was trying to fix my mess, I sat down to do my devotions. In my discouragement, I flipped to Psalm 34, then prayed.

"Lord, I need something this morning. I feel awful. I created more work for my husband even though I was trying to help him. Please give me something from your Word, not just to teach others, but to help me."

When I finished praying, I looked down and read.

Psalm 34:1 "... I will bless the LORD at all times: his praise shall continually be in my mouth."

Immediately I knew that verse was exactly what I needed. Here I was trying to wallow in my pity party pool, and the Spirit of God was showing me I needed to praise the Lord instead. He is worthy of our praise even when things do not go according to our plans. He is worthy of our worship and devotion even when things seem to be falling apart. He is worthy at all times. I do not have time for pity parties.

"But, Lord, how do I switch gears from pity party to praise party?"

I read a little more.

Psalm 34:2-3 "My soul shall make her boast in the LORD: the humble shall hear thereof, and be glad. O magnify the LORD with me, and let us exalt his name together."

We leave the pity party and enter the praise party when we get our eyes of off self and get our eyes back on Him. The guest of honor at a pity party is me. The guest of honor at a praise party is the Lord.

Yes, there are times when we have good intentions and honorable plans that do not work out. We have a choice in our response: pity party or praise party.

This morning I entered the pity party, but then I called out to Him.

> Psalm 34:4 "I sought the LORD, and he heard me, and delivered me from all my fears."

I like this new party much better. The Guest of honor certainly is worthy!

Day 77
Party Invitation (Psalm 34:2-3)

I love parties. I love attending parties and throwing parties. I love the games, the fellowship, the food, and the entertainment of parties. I love the festivities. I love throwing theme parties the best!

I hosted the July Fourth party this year. The theme was Freedom. I set up "breakout/escape" rooms with fun clues to open a lock. That was one of the most fun parties I have ever hosted.

I have to confess that sometimes I throw terrible, ungodly parties. I am not talking about parties with beer or parties with worldly music and such. These parties I throw, though, are still carnal and wicked. I hate it when I realize I have thrown one of those parties. It breaks my heart even more when I realize I have sent out invitations to those parties. (If I send you an invitation to those parties, please respectfully decline to attend.)

Every day, you and I send out invitations to one of two parties. We may not realize we do it. Both parties have the same theme: praise.

The first party has self at the center. When we boast of our accomplishments and talents, we send out an invitation for people to come to a party to praise us.

The second party has the Jesus as the focal point. When we give Him the glory He is due, we send out an invitation for people to join us in praising Him.

You know who will attend the second party? Humble people who love the Lord will come. They love those parties!

> *Psalm 34:2 "My soul shall make her boast in the LORD: the humble shall hear thereof, and be glad. O magnify the LORD with me, and let us exalt his name together."*

When you hear me say, "To God be the glory," I have just sent you an invitation to a Praise Him party. Join me. Let us exalt Him together.

Day 78
Serving and Stealing (Psalm 35)

Sometimes ministry here can be really difficult. I am not talking about the hardships of living here. Yes, sometimes it is difficult because of physical challenges, but there are things we occasionally deal with that are even more taxing to endure emotionally and spiritually.

Just after the first major earthquake a few years ago, we learned quickly how demanding ministry can be. Though we experienced many things firsthand, we also heard stories of things other groups endured. One group went into a village to help build emergency shelters for earthquake victims. While that group was building, people from the village went through the group's vehicles and stole all their tools and supplies. The group was there to selflessly serve the people, and several of the people took advantage of them. I cannot imagine the frustration and heartbreak. That group left the village. Another group, unaware of the previous situation, came in to build and the same thing happened to them.

One time when our group went into a village to help build emergency relief shelters, many people sat around watching them build. As our men worked, several men were mocking them and treating them poorly. Our men were serving and making a difference while others did nothing. Our group kept building and just ignored them. They were not doing it for the people. They were building for the glory of the Lord. It was still heartbreaking.

When you pour your heart into serving others, it cuts deeply to have them take advantage of you or to have them show hatred or disdain for you when you love them and want to help.

David knew what that was like.

> Psalm 35:13-16 "But as for me, when they were sick, my clothing was sackcloth: I humbled my soul with fasting; and my prayer returned into mine own bosom. I behaved myself as though he had been my friend or brother: I bowed down heavily, as one that mourneth for his mother. But in mine adversity they rejoiced, and gathered themselves together: yea, the abjects gathered themselves together against me, and I knew it not; they did tear me, and ceased not: With hypocritical mockers in feasts, they gnashed upon me with their teeth."

When David's enemies were in need, David had compassion. He mourned, prayed, fasted, and treated his enemies like friends and brothers. Then his enemies rewarded him with mockery, false accusations, and cruelty.

David did not retaliate. He did not seek revenge. How did David get through such heartbreak and difficulty with his enemies? How could he endure such treatment?

1. He turned to the Lord and trusted the Lord to handle it. Psalm 35:1 "Plead my cause, O LORD, with them that strive with me: fight against them that fight against me."
2. He rejoiced in the fact that there were people who treasured righteousness. There were people on his side who love God, knew the truth, and supported David. Psalm 35:27 "Let them shout for joy, and be glad, that favour my righteous cause: yea, let them say continually, Let the LORD be magnified, which hath pleasure in the prosperity of his servant."

One day as our group of men worked building shelters, village men sat around mocking them. Our men continued working. Then suddenly, a young woman grabbed some of the supplies and started helping. They showed her how she could help, and she worked as hard as any of our men. It put to shame the men sitting around doing nothing. It also encouraged our group.

When people you try to serve do not treat you with the kindness and compassion you showed them, remind yourself that you do what you do for God's glory, not for their appreciation or reciprocation. Continue to love your enemies, do good to them, and pray for them. Let God fight the battle with them because it is an issue of their hearts. Learn to rejoice in those who love righteousness and treat you with kindness. Do not waste your time stewing over those who live to bring you low.

Day 79
Accurate Perspective (Psalm 36)

My family is originally from western North Carolina. Our home town is surrounded by the beautiful Blue Ridge Mountains. People from all over the world come to see our mountains during the changing of the leaves in the fall season. Words just cannot do justice to the splendor of the colorful canvas of orange, yellow, red, and brown trees that decorate the mountains. We are very proud of our mountains.

When I moved here I gained new perspective. Surrounding the valley where we live now are "mountains" that are the same height and similar shape to our mountains back in North Carolina. The people here, however, call these "mountains" hills. They will laugh at you if you call them mountains, because off into the distance behind these hills is a mountain range that towers high above these tiny mounds of dirt. The majestic white-capped giants are several miles away and still they dominate the hill area as if the hills were nothing more than tiny ant colonies.

It is time to gain a little perspective.

Psalm 36:1-2 "The transgression of the wicked saith within my heart, that there is no fear of God before his eyes. For he flattereth himself in his own eyes, until his iniquity be found to be hateful."

In man's own eyes, he is big. He is in control. He does not need to fear anyone, even God, because he flatters himself with the thoughts of how strong and powerful he is. He boasts and brags. He makes confident plans.

> Psalm 36:3-4 "The words of his mouth are iniquity and deceit: he hath left off to be wise, and to do good. He deviseth mischief upon his bed; he setteth himself in a way that is not good; he abhorreth not evil."

He does not take thought of how little and weak and helpless he really is. He is like a tiny ant in an ant colony and yet he sees himself as Mount Everest. He imagines he is master of the universe. He is big in his own eyes.

And then there is God...

> Psalm 36:5-7 "Thy mercy, O LORD, is in the heavens; and thy faithfulness reacheth unto the clouds. Thy righteousness is like the great mountains; thy judgments are a great deep: O LORD, thou preservest man and beast. How excellent is thy lovingkindness, O God! therefore the children of men put their trust under the shadow of thy wings."

His mercy cannot be contained. His lovingkindness is immeasurable. His righteousness towers high above the works of men. His judgments are deeper than the ocean. His safety covers His children like the wing of a massive eagle casting a great shadow of protection over all those who trust in Him. Our God is big. He is powerful. He is truly in control, and He is worthy of adoration and fear.

Imagine me looking down at a tiny ant hill and calling it a mountain. Imagine me boasting of its greatness and power and majesty. Then imagine me standing at the foot of Mount Everest. I can simply step on the ant hill and collapse its peak without any effort, and yet Mount Everest has only been scaled by a handful of people throughout history. It has claimed many lives in their attempt to reach its summit. Even the most skilled climbers respect the dangers the deadly high peak poses to its challengers.

Who are we to boast in ourselves and make confident plans? Who are we to flatter ourselves thinking we have power and control? We are but tiny ants totally dependent on His mercy, lovingkindness, righteousness, judgments, and protection. God is big, and it is prudent for us to learn the fear of the Lord.

Day 80
The TDCR Battle Plan (Psalm 37)

With my oldest child starting Boot Camp in the US Army in a few weeks, my mind has been on military lately. I guess that is a pretty good mindset to have when reading through Psalms. So much of it deals with battles and enemies. David was an amazing military leader.

Every good military has a battle plan. Every good military leader communicates that battle plan to his soldiers. He does not tell his soldiers the whole story, but he fills them in on the part they are responsible to carry out. The leader gives precise instructions and the soldiers must follow those instructions in order to win the battle.

In life, we face many battles as Christians. The good thing is that our Commanding Officer, the Lord, has given us precise instructions on how to fight the battles. He has not told us the entirety of His plan, but He has guaranteed us the victory if we follow His instructions.

The TDCR Battle Plan

Trust

> Psalm 37:3 "Trust in the LORD, and do good; so shalt thou dwell in the land, and verily thou shalt be fed."

The first part of the battle plan is to trust our Commanding Officer. Trust what?

- That He knows the battle
- That He has the perfect plan
- That He is in control
- That He is powerful enough to carry out His plan

Delight

> Psalm 37:4 "Delight thyself also in the
> LORD; and he shall give thee the desires
> of thine heart."

One of the greatest tactics of any enemy is divide and conquer. If the enemy can weasel his way in between the soldiers and the commander, he can create confusion. We have to be vigilant about this strategy. The Lord must be our delight. He must be our heart, our focus, our everything! He must be what brings us joy. He must be what we anticipate and look forward to. He cannot simply be a peripheral part of our lives, off to the sidelines. He must be central.

Commit

> Psalm 37:5 "Commit thy way unto the
> LORD; trust also in him; and he shall
> bring it to pass."

To win this battle, the battle must start with a surrender. It is a complete surrender of our lives to Him. Our will, our desires, our goals, and our decisions must be placed in His hands. How can we do that? Trust. A person who does not trust God will keep holding the reins of his life. He will refuse to hand those reins over to the Lord.

Rest

> Psalm 37:7 "Rest in the LORD, and wait patiently for him: fret not thyself because of him who prospereth in his way, because of the man who bringeth wicked devices to pass."

It is not enough to wait on the Lord. We should wait on the Lord, but how we wait is just as important as the waiting. He does not want us wasting energy pacing back and forth, fretting while we wait. He wants us to rest. He wants us to grab a spiritual cup of hot tea, sit down, and rest. He really is in control and there is no need for us to worry. We need to wait patiently. He will accomplish His part of the Battle Plan. We need to accomplish our part.

Trust, Delight, Commit, Rest. That is our battle plan. That is our strategy. That is the command given by our Commanding Officer.

Day 81
Pricks, Kicks, and Cuts (Psalm 38)

True confession: Going to the doctor does not scare me. Getting shots does not frighten me. Having my blood drawn for blood work does not bother me. Do you want to know what I struggle with when visiting the doctor's office? Do you know those spring-loaded lancets? They are the finger poking instruments the nurses use to prick the tip of the finger. The spring-loaded ones are conveniently cocked and ready. The nurse simply has to touch the release button as the lancet is placed firmly on the fingertip. With a distinct, loud click the lancet shoots the blade into the tip of the finger.

Why does that bother me? Every time I hear that click noise I jump. It startles me. No matter how much I am expecting the noise and try to relax, when I hear that loud click I jump. When a blade is being shot into the skin, that is not the best time to jump.

One day I went to visit the doctor. I had to have my finger pricked. I told the nurse, "You need to hold my hand tightly, because when I hear that click I will jump." I made it a habit to warn nurses who were using the spring-loaded lancets. Nurses could then take a death-grip on my hand and proceed without incident.

Unfortunately, this one nurse did not take my warning seriously. She held my hand, pressed the release button on the lancet, the click sounded it is deadly intent, and I jumped. What should have been a simple, small prick was now a nasty cut that sliced across the tip of my finger. Pricks turn to cuts when you jerk away.

> Psalm 38:2 *"For thine arrows stick fast in me, and thy hand presseth me sore."*

David was being pricked. The arrows of the Lord's conviction were sticking him. It was uncomfortable. David did not jerk away. David did not reject. David knew God was doing a healing work in his heart. He needed the conviction and the chastisement because he had sinned. How did David respond?

> Psalm 38:18 *"For I will declare mine iniquity; I will be sorry for my sin."*

David repented.

> Acts 2:37 *"Now when they heard this, they were pricked in their heart, and said unto Peter and to the rest of the apostles, Men and brethren, what shall we do?"*

When the people of Acts 2 heard Peter's message, they were pricked in their hearts. The Gospel convicted them, and they responded with repentance.

Later in the book of Acts the high priest, the chief priests, and the captain of the officers gave a much different response. They heard the truth about Christ. Peter and the apostles refused to stop preaching Jesus.

Acts 5:33 "When they heard that, they were cut to the heart, and took counsel to slay them."

They were not just pricked. They were cut! The same sword (God's Word) that pricked the people of Acts 2 cut the heart of these men because they jerked away. They rejected. They were not interested in the healing that the Lord was offering.

Stephen preached the Gospel in Acts 7 and received a similar response.

Acts 7:54 "When they heard these things, they were cut to the heart, and they gnashed on him with their teeth."

Those men to whom he preached rejected God's Word, and Stephen became the first martyr.

Standing close by, consenting to his martyrdom, was a man named Saul. Saul was vicious in his pursuit and threats against Christians, but God was already working in Saul's heart. On the outside, he was dedicated and determined, yet God's Word was pricking his heart. When he met Jesus on the road to Damascus, Jesus confronted Saul about his response to the pricks.

Acts 9:5 "And he said, Who art thou, Lord? And the Lord said, I am Jesus whom thou persecutest: it is hard for thee to kick against the pricks."

He was not rejecting God's work in his heart. He was not cut to the heart, but he was kicking. Later he submitted to the pricks and repented. He responded to the conviction of the Holy Spirit.

What are you doing when the Word of God pricks? How do you respond to conviction? Do you jerk away and reject? It will cut your heart and make you angry and bitter. It will cause you to lash out at those who speak the truth of God's Word. Do you kick against the pricks? Do you fight the work God is doing, or do you, like David, submit to conviction?

Psalm 38:18 "For I will declare mine iniquity; I will be sorry for my sin."

Day 82
Fire Within (Psalm 39)

David knew exactly how we feel. Something gets said that is not right. Maybe it is inaccurate. Maybe it is insulting. Maybe it is offensive. Maybe it is said intentionally. You get a little heated. You just want to respond. As your heart burns within you, the temptations come.

- Having the last word
- Telling someone off
- Setting the record straight
- Sarcasm
- Passive aggressive talk
- Social media arguments
- Proving your point

> *Psalm 39:3 "My heart was hot within me,*
> *while I was musing the fire burned..."*

Yes, David knew how we feel, but what did David do?

> *Psalm 39:1 "I said, I will take heed to my*
> *ways, that I sin not with my tongue: I will*
> *keep my mouth with a bridle, while the*
> *wicked is before me."*

David held his tongue. He knew the battle was the Lord's, not his. He knew it was not his job to defend himself or to bring the enemy low from his lofty perch.

What is it that makes us get into arguments on social media? What is it that drives us to verbally humble those who speak ill of us? Pride. David knew this was a temptation for him. He chose to keep silence altogether. It was not that he did not say bad things. He did not even speak good things because he knew those things would have been said in pride.

Psalm 39:2 "I was dumb with silence, I held my peace, even from good; and my sorrow was stirred."

David finally broke his silence, but notice who he addressed:

Psalm 39:3-4 "My heart was hot within me, while I was musing the fire burned: then spake I with my tongue, LORD, make me to know mine end, and the measure of my days, what it is; that I may know how frail I am."

He did not speak to the enemy. He spoke to the Lord. He asked the Lord to humble him and to help him battle his pride. He lumped himself in the same group as every other person and called himself vanity.

Psalm 39:5 "Behold, thou hast made my days as an handbreadth; and mine age is as nothing before thee: verily every man at his best state is altogether vanity. Selah."

He was declaring that he was no better than his enemy. He was just as vain and just as needy as all other men.

Are you struggling to keep your silence? Are you tempted to react to someone's attack? Is your heart burning within you?

Psalm 39:7 "And now, Lord, what wait I for? my hope is in thee."

Wait for the Lord. Turn to Him. Remind yourself that you, too, are weak, sinful, and needy. Humble yourself.

"If any man thinks ill of you, do not be angry with him, for you are worse than he thinks you to be." -Charles H Spurgeon

Day 83
From Pit to Rock (Psalm 40:2)

There is a scary phenomenon that happens here during monsoon season. The streets are full of danger on a normal day, but during monsoon the dangers reach a new level of peril. One day while driving my scooter on a paved road, I reached a section covered by a large puddle. My daughter was riding on the scooter behind me. The rain was pouring down, and we were ready to get home and get dry.

I slowed down and started driving through the puddle. Halfway through the twenty foot pond, the front tire of my scooter suddenly plunged into a deep, unseen hole. The scooter came to an instant stop, slinging me into the handlebars of the scooter and slinging my daughter into my back. I was able to keep us from toppling over, but my feet were soaked in the muddy water. It took some effort, but I was able to get the scooter out of the hole. My hips and waist, however, were sore and bruised from the sudden jolt and stop. I was happy to be on firm ground after that.

> Psalm 40:2 *"He brought me up also out of an horrible pit, out of the miry clay, and set my feet upon a rock, and established my goings."*

David was excited about getting on firm ground too. He was in a pit that caused pain and agony. God lifted him out of that pit and put David on firm ground.

If we are saved, God has done the same for us. He has set us on a firm foundation. He has set us on a new path. We are new creatures in Christ. Having assurance of salvation is powerful. Knowing that I am out of the pit and established on the Rock helps me to walk confidently in Him. He has established my goings on this new path and has even given me clear instructions on how to navigate this new path.

I will never again walk on that old path because He removed me completely from it. Sometimes, however, my walk mimics how I used to walk on that old path. It is during those times that I need to remind myself where He brought me from, as well as where He placed me now.

Do you remember the pit you were in? Do you remember the day He lifted you up out of the pit? Are you on the new path walking confidently in Him because you are sure of your salvation? Are you walking on the new path, but acting like you are still on the old path?

Day 84

What Does He Want? (Psalm 40)

I love Christmas time. It is a very festive season in our home. I try to put some form of Christmas in every room of the house. Christmas towels, Christmas wreaths, Christmas candles, Christmas pine cones, Christmas blankets and pillows, Christmas bows, and Christmas garland. It is like a Christmas explosion!

Decorating for Christmas is something I enjoy and have gotten pretty good at doing, but there is something I struggle doing during the Christmas season. I am terrible at it. I am disasterous at buying Christmas gifts. When Christmas rolls around, it is like I have forgotten everything I ever knew about a person. My mind goes blank. I have no idea what to get them.

My husband, on the other hand, is the most amazing gift giver. He always seems to come up with the perfect gift. It is not just the gift that he gets that excites me. It is the heart and attitude with which he gets the gift. He gets so excited! He carefully picks out presents based on what he knows about the person. He hunts and hunts until he finds exactly what he is looking for. When he gives the gift, he stands there with a big grin on his face, staring and waiting for the person's reaction. When the person bubbles over with joy, my husband's face lights up like a Christmas tree. You would think he was the one who received the gift.

*Psalm 40:6 "Sacrifice and offering thou
didst not desire; mine ears hast thou
opened: burnt offering and sin offering
hast thou not required."*

What does God want? What gift is He looking to receive? When He opens our gifts to Him, what is He looking for? Is He looking for an obligatory gift? Is He pleased when we give Him something that we feel we have to give out of necessity?

- The mandatory church attendance and the required offering in the offering plate
- The unavoidable song as everyone stands in the congregation
- The compulsory prayer before a meal or before bed
- The quickly read verse done out of necessity

Have you ever received a gift that you knew the person only gave because they felt they had to give something? It was not heartfelt. It was merely given out of a sense of obligation. I have received those kinds of gifts. I have also given them many times. It makes me feel shallow, and it should.

What makes my husband such a great gift giver?

1) My husband thinks about the person, who they are, and what matters to them.

When we give to the Lord, we need to do the same thing. What is God like? What matters to Him?

Psalm 40:5 "Many, O LORD my God, are
thy wonderful works which thou hast
done, and thy thoughts which are to us-
ward: they cannot be reckoned up in
order unto thee: if I would declare and
speak of them, they are more than can
be numbered."

Do we realize how much God thinks about us? Do we realize how much He does for us every day? Do we realize what He has already done for us? He dotes on us. He treasures us and loves us deeply. What kind of gifts would matter to Him?

2) My husband gives out of a desire to please the receiver of the gift.

Psalm 40:8 "I delight to do thy will, O my
God: yea, thy law is within my heart."

David did not do things out of obligation. He delighted in pleasing the Lord. It was in his heart. It was his passion and desire. It was not just the gift that mattered. It is the heart with which he gave the gift.

What gifts does our God want? What is His desire? He wants us. He wants our hearts. He wants us to delight in Him and in serving Him.

When my husband gives me a gift, I certainly enjoy the gift, but what I enjoy more than anything is seeing the joy and excitement plastered across his face as he gives the gift. His heart is in it because he loves me.

What does our Father in Heaven want? He does not want us just to sing. He wants us to wholeheartedly praise Him in song.

Psalm 40:3 "And he hath put a new song
in my mouth, even praise unto our God:
many shall see it, and fear, and shall
trust in the LORD."

He does not want us to just sacrifice and give offerings. He wants us to delight in serving Him. He wants to look on our faces and our hearts and see our joy as we give to Him gifts of love, praise, trust, and service.

Do we give Him obligatory gifts, or are we searching out the perfect gifts to give to Him with joy?

Day 85
Hugging Through Dirt (Psalm 41:1-2)

I love my children's class sweethearts. Sometimes they are a wild bunch. Sometimes it is a crazy mix of ages and languages. They are often full of smiles and giggles. Sometimes their clothes are ripped. They are often dirty. They do not notice or care. They are just happy to be in children's class, singing "Read Your Bible" and laughing as they mimic growing like a plant.

All of my sweethearts are from families in such poverty that the American mind cannot fathom. Even many of the American homeless are better off than the majority of these families. They work in farming and agriculture and make just enough money to put the cheapest of foods on their plates. Many live in one room shacks right in the middle of the garden that they tend for the land owner.

I look in my shoe cabinet and see more than a dozen pairs of shoes. I have warm weather shoes, cold weather shoes, shoes to match black outfits, shoes to match brown outfits, running shoes, biking shoes, aerobics shoes, and bedroom shoes. Most of these people have one pair of shoes: cheap and flimsy flip flops that they wear year-round, in cold weather, hot weather, monsoon rains, and in all activities. They work in the fields in them, play soccer in them, walk to church in them, and walk to school in them.

Psalm 41:1 "Blessed is he that
considereth the poor: the LORD will
deliver him in time of trouble. The LORD
will preserve him, and keep him alive;
and he shall be blessed upon the earth:
and thou wilt not deliver him unto the
will of his enemies."

It is easy to throw money at these situations to try to solve their problems. There is something much more difficult, though. Would you give hugs and love on them through all the dirt? Would you let these sweet faces crawl up in your lap even on the days they smell like urine? Would you play with them and teach them and correct them day after day even when they can do nothing for you in return? Would you hug the mom even with the threat of lice looming with every physical contact?

Yes, sometimes money does make an impact. Recently a woman sent us a substantial amount of money to minister to the children. She heard about them from ten thousand miles away, and her heart was broken. I think she would have let every one of them crawl up in her lap, and she would have snuggled with each one as if they were her own grandchildren, dirt and all!

We took the money and bought these precious babies much needed winter clothing. (They had absolutely nothing, and the temperatures were dropping.) The kids were thrilled, and so were the parents who could not properly clothe their own children.

The children's biggest thrill, however, is that the "rich man" and his "high caste" partner play with them and love them. They know there is something special about this because in their culture, rich people and high caste people have nothing to do with poor, low caste people.

When you see the homeless man on the street, do you turn the other way? Is he too vile and dirty for your time and affection? When the drunk bum on the road staggers along through life, do you continue your Christmas shopping without thought of his eternity? Are you focused on your shopping and getting more and more stuff for yourself, your family, and your friends? Are you so busy with the season of giving and cheer that you have no time for ministering to those who have the greatest need? Are you showing them the Saviour? Are you reaching out to them, and especially reaching out to their greatest need, the need of salvation?

God shows great favor to those who consider the poor. After all, that is what He did for us. When we show love and affection for the poor, we demonstrate the character of God to the world around us. It is more than just throwing money at them. It is getting down in the dirt with them and removing the lines that separate us, just like Jesus did. He reached out to us. We were poor and dirty with sin, and He invited us to crawl up in His lap. He did not just give money to solve our physical problems. He spent time among us meeting the needs of our hearts, souls, and lives.

What are you doing to show the love and compassion of our Saviour to those who are the lowest in our culture? Are you reaching them with the Gospel?

Day 86
Christmas, Cheddar, Pickles, and a Cow (Psalm 42)

When we first moved here, I made a huge mistake. As we were packing to move overseas, our luggage space was limited. We had to prioritize. I made the decision that we did not need to bring Christmas decorations. It really did not seem like a big deal at the time. We have never been overly sentimental. One year we barely did any decorating and we did not seem to mind. One year we did not even put up a Christmas tree, and the kids never said a word, so it seemed like a good thing to leave the Christmas decorations in the States.

When we arrived in our new country in November, we made a mad dash to get the new house set up. Before we knew it, December was at our doorstep. That is when my mistake glared as bright as tacky Christmas lights. It was Christmas time, and yet nothing looked like Christmas. The people here do not celebrate Christmas, so every store looked bare. Every house looked plain. Everything looked like it does every other day of the year. Christmas decor was nowhere to be found and we suddenly felt homesick.

Sometimes you do not realize how much you love something until it is not there. It sounds silly, but we once endured a cheddar cheese shortage here. It went on for seven months. People just do not realize how addicted to cheddar cheese Americans are. I am surprised our blood is not cheddar cheese yellow.

Yes, I whined a little. Do not even let me begin telling you about the dill pickle shortage that has been going on for two years. Those things are not even necessary, just precious to my American taste buds.

My daughter and I love to go running. We have worked up to running 10k. Our next goal is to run a half marathon. Yes, that means she and I are only half crazy. One time we were out running a 10k. It was a hot day, and I had forgotten to bring money with me to grab a bottled water for when we finished our run. At the end of the run, we were panting and parched. The walk home was as excruciating as the 10k run. We sent a text to my husband asking him to meet us at the gate with water. I do not think I have ever been so thirsty! It was foolish and dangerous for us to make such a trip without sufficient means of hydration.

Next door to our home, the neighbors keep a milk cow. They often keep it on a short five-foot rope that runs through its nose and ties it to a stake in the small plot of land. Sometimes they even keep it locked up in a metal shed in the heat of the summer. The poor cow must be roasting in that shed! We always know when it becomes unbearable for the cow. It begins to cry loudly for water. It will continue begging and braying for hours until someone satisfies its thirst.

Psalm 42:1 "As the hart panteth after the water brooks, so panteth my soul after thee, O God. My soul thirsteth for God, for the living God: when shall I come and appear before God?"

Imagine a deer on the run in the heat of the summer. It longs for the safety and the refreshing of the water brooks. As it is being pursued, thirst begins to build. Its mouth becomes dry. Muscles tired and aching, heart pounding, it finally cries out for water.

Do we long for God like that? When it seems He is hiding behind the lattice and we cannot find Him, do we cry out for Him? Do we long for His safety, comfort, and refreshing? He is not like a cheddar cheese shortage or a pickle shortage. We can survive without those. They are nice to have and we love them, but they can be replaced with other things. He is more than just Christmas decorations that we enjoy and miss when they are gone. He is like water. He is vital to life. He is vital to day-to-day survival. I can live without cheddar for at least seven months and pickles for two years and counting. I can even live without the homey feel of Christmas décor, but without water, I am doomed. He is necessary for every day and every minute.

Is He precious to me like my Christmas decorations? Do I miss Him when I realize our fellowship is broken because of sin? When He is silent, do I long to hear His voice?

Do I have an appetite for Him like my beautiful, golden cheddar cheese treasure? Do I hunger for the taste of His goodness and for the buffet of His righteousness and holy character and nature?

Do I realize how vital He is? Do I realize how much I need Him every moment? Do I call out for Him? Do I cry for Him?

Day 87
Uneasy (Psalm 43)

Have you ever had those moments or days when you feel overwhelmed? There is an uneasiness in your spirit. Loads of decisions and responsibilities weigh upon your shoulders. You are not quite sure how to explain that feeling, but it shows up on your face.

This morning I woke up already tired from a difficult and interrupted night of sleep. Responsibilities weigh upon me. Decisions need to be made soon. The load of ministry, motherhood, and the work in the home is a little overwhelming right now. All this is compounded by the emotional strain of being away from my oldest child for Christmas for the first time and a beloved dog that looms on the brink of death.

I sat down to spend my morning quiet time with the Lord. I prayed and asked, "Lord, please send me something. I need to hear from you this morning."

Psalm 43:5 "Why art thou cast down, O my soul? and why art thou disquieted within me?"

David knew how to describe that feeling. He gave it a perfect name.

DISQUIETED: Made uneasy or restless; disturbed; harassed.

Yes, my soul is disquieted within me. I am sure you have been there, too. The key is knowing what to do in those situations. Psalm 43 gives a perfect prescription for the ailment.

1. **Turn to our best resource.**
   Psalm 43:2 "For thou art the God of my strength..."
   God is our source of strength. When my responsibilities are too much for me and my to-do list is too big, they are not too big for Him!

   Psalm 43:5 "... hope in God..."
   God is our source of hope. As my heart feels heavy over the prospect of losing our sweet German Shepherd, I know that God is a great hope and comfort.

   Psalm 43:5 "... for I shall yet praise him, who is the health of my countenance, and my God."
   God is our source of healing and can put a genuine smile on our faces again when we make Him our focus instead of our problems. David turned to praising the Lord. As I long to see my son, I know that I do not have to paste a fake smile on my face. I am too blessed! I have real reasons to smile, and they are all because of my Father who loves me.

2. **Do not make emotional decisions.**
   Psalm 43:3 "O send out thy light and thy truth: let them lead me; let them bring me unto thy holy hill, and to thy tabernacles."
   David did not allow his emotions to guide his steps. He wanted God's truth to lead him. He sought God's direction.

It is amazing how timely God's Word is. The answers to our problems are all right there if we stay faithful to reading His Word and going to Him in prayer. I already feel the weight of my disquieted soul dissipating. Why? My circumstances have not changed. I am still tired from a frustrating night of sleep. I still have responsibilities hanging over my head, but somehow His Word has refocused me. My vision is no longer focused on the cloud. My eyes are again fixed upon the Son.

Day 88
Story Tellers (Psalm 44:1)

One of my favorite things about where we live is that we always have a story to tell. We could talk for hours about how God worked in amazing ways. We could tell you of the time God saved me from being launched off my scooter when I drove over an open manhole. We could tell you how God used a devastating earthquake to open doors for ministry. We could tell you how God saved a man out of Hinduism six weeks before his death. We had been sharing the Gospel with him for years. We could go on and on.

I love reading biographies of great men and women of God who the Lord used throughout history. The men and women were not anything special, but they served an amazing God who changed their lives and then used them in His service.

> Psalm 44:1 "We have heard with our ears, O God, our fathers have told us, what work thou didst in their days, in the times of old."

David loved stories, too. He loved hearing how God worked throughout the history of his people. Generation to generation, the stories were passed down. There were stories of battles like the battle of Jericho. There were stories about God parting waters like the Red Sea. There were stories of manna that fed the people in the wilderness. Oh, how David loved those stories!

David, however, longed for more stories of his own. He loved the story of how God defeated the giant Goliath. He loved the story of the time God helped him kill a lion and bear. They were great stories and they were his own testimonies of God's great power working in his life. David did not want those stories to be his last stories. He wanted God to work in his life every day! He did not want stories about his own greatness. He wanted stories about God working in impossible situations so that God would get all the glory.

> Psalm 44:6 "For I will not trust in my bow, neither shall my sword save me."

> Psalm 44:8 "In God we boast all the day long, and praise thy name for ever. Selah."

Do you have stories of God working in amazing ways? If you are not faithfully in the battle, your stories will be limited. You will have to keep telling the same story over and over about how God worked twenty years ago. If you want fresh and exciting stories, you will have to quit sitting on the sidelines. People who are in the battle daily will have daily battlefield stories of God's goodness, grace, and glory.

People on the sidelines are satisfied with telling other people's stories of how amazing God is. People in the battle daily are encouraged by other people's stories, but they also are zealous about sharing their own stories. They love seeing God work in their lives personally.

I want to be one of those people. I want to be on the battlefield experiencing God doing great things in and through me. I want to be a storyteller with something to say. I want to be able to boast and brag on my God all day long about things He is doing in my life personally.

"Expect great things from God. Attempt great things for God." — William Carey

---

Day 89
Peeling Paint and Fading Glory (Psalm 45)

I love the Biltmore Estate in Asheville, North Carolina. My husband and I have been privileged to go there twice. It is an exquisite mansion, and its splendor and beauty are captivating. It is grand and breathtaking, but I have a confession. When I went through the Biltmore House both times, I not only enjoyed the charm of its expensive furnishings and history, but I also looked for reminders of its temporary nature.

I loved the massive curtains, but I also noticed where a few were worn or slightly faded. I loved the wallpapers, but I also noticed there were occasional spots where the paper was beginning to curl at the corners. I loved the paint, but there were places where paint had begun to chip and peel. As magnificent as this house is, it (like everything else on the earth) is a temporary kingdom. It is fading. It requires an enormous amount of effort for its upkeep, and yet it is a losing battle.

In Psalm 45, David is captivated by the majesty of God. He is focused on God as King. His words describe the Lord's power, royalty, majesty, and sovereignty. His speech indites (gushes in words) the matter of just how regal, righteous, and pure God the King is.

Psalm 45:3 "Gird thy sword upon thy thigh, O most mighty, with thy glory and

thy majesty. And in thy majesty ride
prosperously because of truth and
meekness and righteousness; and thy
right hand shall teach thee terrible
things."

I was captivated by the splendor of a place that was fading and faltering-- a place that would one day fall away. Its temporary nature showed through in spots. David was captivated by the eternal, unfading, unfaltering King whose kingdom would never decay and fall away. His throne will never chip, crack, peel, or crumble.

Psalm 45:6 "Thy throne, O God, is for
ever and ever: the sceptre of thy
kingdom is a right sceptre."

Though we may find a sense of beauty, wonder, and awe in earthly abodes that fade away, let us never lose our sense of awe in the King and kingdom which will stand in all its perfect glory forever. Let us take time to ponder and meditate upon His glory and majesty.

Day 90
Unmovable (Psalm 46)

Enduring a major earthquake was difficult, but the most devastating and frightening part of it was not buildings falling, people screaming, and the horrible rumbling. Those things were scary, most certainly, but the most frightening thing was more fundamental than that. It took a while for my mind to begin processing it. The most frightening part was the ground which had been stable and secure my whole life was moving and no longer dependable.

From the moment I was born, the earth beneath me was steady and sure. I walked with confidence on it from the day I learned to walk. I jumped, skipped, hopped, rolled, ran, and crawled on a firm foundation of dirt, grass, and rock miles deep and seemingly impenetrable. On April 25, 2015, the truth that I had believed my whole life was shattered and revealed as a lie. The ground could indeed move and shake violently.

It is difficult to explain the mental and emotional strain I endured trying to process this new fact. The human mind will struggle to comprehend such a radical notion. Such challenges are what create things like PTSD (post-traumatic stress disorder.) Yes, our family still deals with PTSD.

Psalm 46:1-3 "God is our refuge and strength, a very present help in trouble. Therefore will not we fear, though the earth be removed, and

*though the mountains be carried into the
midst of the sea; Though the waters
thereof roar and be troubled, though the
mountains shake with the swelling
thereof. Selah."*

The truth is that even the earth beneath our feet is unreliable for safety. We cannot count on it. The mountains move and shake. They can be removed. We experienced that, too, as we saw landslides that wiped out entire mountain sides, covering and burying entire villages. (These verses in Psalm 46 never meant so much to me as they do now after the earthquake.) We do not have to fear, though. Why?

Man's kingdoms can be shaken, removed, and destroyed.

*Psalm 46:6 "The heathen raged, the
kingdoms were moved: he uttered his
voice, the earth melted."*

Man often acts like he is invincible, but no matter how strong the military, no matter how strong the government, no matter how strong the economy, and no matter how strong the people, any country is vulnerable. Any country and people can be removed. A simple shake of the ground, a devastating storm, a cunning enemy.

But God's kingdom?

Psalm 46:5 "God is in the midst of her;
she shall not be moved: God shall help
her, and that right early."

God is stable. His kingdom is unmovable. His throne is impenetrable. Unlike the day when my trust in the ground beneath me was shattered, the reliability of God will never change. That is what makes Him the best refuge and help in our times of trouble. He is unchanging and immovable. That is why we can be still. That is why we can run to Him in confidence. When we stand upon Him and His truth we are standing on a firm foundation that will never be shaken. It will never be moved. It is even more solid and trustworthy of a foundation than the very earth we walk upon.

Psalm 46:10-11 "Be still, and know that I
am God: I will be exalted among the
heathen, I will be exalted in the
earth. The LORD of hosts is with us; the
God of Jacob is our refuge. Selah."

Day 91
Indoor Voices? No, Thank You (Psalm 47)

"Indoor voices!" I said it over and over again to our children when they were young. There is something about young children. When they get excited, their volume goes up to a feverish pitch. Sometimes their excessive volume is an irritation to me, but most times it makes me giggle. You can almost see their excitement and joy emanating from their bodies in waves of sound. It takes a while to teach them the time and the place for being noisy, especially when I sometimes am guilty, too. I get excited and my volume button goes up!

Recently, we had a couple of younger children staying with us at our home. I found myself again saying that familiar command, "Indoor voices, please." They would be quieter for just a few sentences, but then their excitement would build as they told some amazing and thrilling story. Their little bodies would wiggle as they continued talking and the tension began building. Before they knew it, their volume was once again on overload as they smiled, giggled, and of course shouted their story with glee.

Psalm 47 is not saying, "Indoor voices, please." It is saying, "Turn the volume up, you guys! It is time to praise!"

Psalm 47:1 "O clap your hands, all ye people; shout unto God with the voice of triumph."

Does God excite you? When you and I sit and think about the God we serve, it should create a rise in volume as if we were children getting excited about a story we want to tell. Maybe we have lost our "praise voices" and opted for "indoor voices" because we have forgotten to dwell on the goodness of God. We have forgotten to think about the attributes of our Father. We have neglected meditating and studying about how amazing our Saviour Jesus is. We have lost our song. We have lost our shout. We have opted for polite indoor voices when He is worthy of our excitement-driven noise.

Psalm 47:5-7 "God is gone up with a shout, the LORD with the sound of a trumpet. Sing praises to God, sing praises: sing praises unto our King, sing praises. For God is the King of all the earth: sing ye praises with understanding."

Day 92
As They Pass By (Psalm 48)

Every day, thousands of people pass by our church. I wonder what they say? Every day, thousands of people pass in front of our home. They know the foreigners live here. I wonder what they say. I wonder what our neighbors say to each other when we are not around. I wonder what they say when we pass by their shops.

We carry the name of Christ, so what they think of us will also impact their thoughts of God.

Jerusalem, Mount Zion, was the city where God chose to place His name.

Psalm 48:2 "Beautiful for situation, the joy of the whole earth, is mount Zion, on the sides of the north, the city of the great King."

As people thought of Jerusalem, so were their thoughts of God. At the time this Psalm was written, people had a respect for God. They feared Him. As enemies or outsiders passed by Jerusalem, they would hasten their steps. They knew God was with the people of Jerusalem.

Psalm 48:4-6 "For, lo, the kings were assembled, they passed by together. They saw it, and so they marvelled; they were troubled, and

hasted away. Fear took hold upon them
there, and pain, as of a woman in
travail."

We are Christians. Jesus's name is attached to us. People know it. What makes a difference is when they know we have been with Him and He is with us.

Acts 4:12-13 "Neither is there salvation in
any other: for there is none other name
under heaven given among men,
whereby we must be saved. Now when
they saw the boldness of Peter and John,
and perceived that they were unlearned
and ignorant men, they marvelled; and
they took knowledge of them, that they
had been with Jesus."

When people pass by us, do they fear and have respect because of our God? Have we carried the name of Christ in such a manner that they have something to respect? Are we spending time with Jesus so that His holy scent permeates our lives and His power is clearly seen working and moving in and through us? Are we living in such a way that people see Jesus and not us?

As people passed by Jerusalem, they were not afraid of the military might. They were petrified of the fact that God was there, and He was with His people. What do people see when they pass by me?

Day 93
Dead Dog (Psalm 49)

This week has been a tough week. Our beloved German Shepherd, Chief, had to be put down. At a young five years of age, he was in poor health. He was unable to stand or walk. He had lost all control of his bladder. We had fought so hard to save him for months, but it was a losing battle. There was nothing else that could be done. Tears were shed, and we said goodbye. Our hearts were broken. Chief was a dog, not like a human who is made in the image of God, but he was such a treasured part of our family. He was a special gift from the Lord, and we are thankful for every day that he was with us. He will be missed.

However, this week somewhere a parent died, a child was lost, a spouse was taken, a baby was miscarried. This week people somewhere cried and said goodbyes to family members or friends. This week somewhere people received a phone call they never imagined they would receive. This week the truth was inescapable. All people, young and old, rich or poor, educated or simple-- we will all face death.

Psalm 49:10 "For he seeth that wise men die, likewise the fool and the brutish person perish, and leave their wealth to others."

The fact is that we are all going to die. It is unavoidable. There is no way around it. No one can buy their way out of death. They cannot buy the way of loved ones out of death.

> *Psalm 49:7 "None of them can by any*
> *means redeem his brother, nor give to*
> *God a ransom for him:"*

We cannot ransom ourselves or anyone else with money or good works or religious deeds. We are all in the same boat heading toward death, and we are all worthy of death because of our sin.

> *Psalm 49:5 "Wherefore should I fear in*
> *the days of evil, when the iniquity of my*
> *heels shall compass me about?"*

We are all surrounded by our own iniquity. I cannot pay for anyone else's sin, nor can I free them from death's quicksand because I am facing the same fate. I am being dragged toward death just like you are, because we are sinners. The payment for sin is death.

> *Psalm 49:14 "Like sheep they are laid in*
> *the grave; death shall feed on them; and*
> *the upright shall have dominion over*
> *them in the morning; and their beauty*
> *shall consume in the grave from their*
> *dwelling."*

We cannot take anything with us either. All the pursuits of this world are vanity. When we are laid in the grave, those temporal pursuits will vanish.

> *Psalm 49:17 "For when he dieth he shall carry nothing away: his glory shall not descend after him."*

This Psalm seems sad and depressing, but there is hope.

> *Psalm 49:15 "But God will redeem my soul from the power of the grave: for he shall receive me. Selah."*

There is but one hope. That hope is for God to receive us. That hope is for God to redeem us from the power of the grave. How do we know if we are one of the ones who will be received? How do we know if we are one of the redeemed ones who will have victory over the grave?

We are one of the redeemed when we have turned from trusting our riches or our own righteousness, and instead have trusted God's plan of salvation. God sent His Son to pay for our sins. Jesus died for us. We cannot give a ransom for ourselves or for each other because we are guilty, but Jesus, the sinless and perfect Son of God could ransom us with His own blood.

If we have called out to God for forgiveness with a heart of repentance and if we have trusted in the death, burial, and resurrection of Jesus as a payment for our sin, we become one of those who will be received by God. We become one of those that are called the redeemed. Death no longer has a sting to it because we will have victory.

The fact is that we are all heading toward death, but the question is, are you ready? Are you one of the redeemed?

Day 94
Say the Magic Words (Psalm 51:16-17)

I have learned more about myself and about my God through parenting than I ever imagined possible. I am more like my children than I realize. I remember when I was younger I did many of the same things my children do now. My children are not any different than anyone else's children. They all have the same sin nature.

My youngest child loves aggravating. He finds irritating others a great sense of amusement. My oldest child is the boss, controller, manipulator, and drama queen. You can imagine the fireworks this created when he and the youngest child were growing up under the same roof.

The middle child is the sneaky one. She is good at flying under the parenting radar. She knows how to get to her two brothers without stirring up trouble for herself. She is not controlled by emotions and uses her head before acting. Parenting these three has been an adventure.

Needless to say, the two boys, oil and water that they are, created the most friction. One would stir up trouble and the other would turn up the volume. I would try to intervene. At some point I would tell them to apologize to each other. Sometimes the apology was slightly less than sincere. The guilty child would roll his eyes, sigh, and in a patronizing tone blurt out, "Sorry!" Oh, how that would drive me crazy! The child obeyed, but the heart was far from truly being repentant.

Psalm 51:16-17 "For thou desirest not sacrifice; else would I give it: thou delightest not in burnt offering. The sacrifices of God are a broken spirit: a broken and a contrite heart, O God, thou wilt not despise."

In the Old Testament, God had commanded the children of Israel to sacrifice animals as a covering for sin. It was a temporary plan until the promised Saviour, Jesus, was sent. David was not saying that sacrifices were unnecessary during that time period. He was saying that the sacrifice of animals was not the focus of what God wanted to teach. It was not the goal or God's desire and longing. God desired a humble, repentant heart, not empty religious acts.

When I was disciplining my children, I was not focused on getting them to say the words "I'm sorry" as if those words were some kind of magic sin eraser. "Quick! You sinned against your brother. Say the words!" My desire for them was that they would see their sin and see their broken fellowship. My desire was that they would be repentant. It was a heart issue, and I was after the heart.

How many times have the words "forgive me of my sins" rolled off my tongue, but my heart was not sincere nor repentant? How many times have I treated prayer like a magic Etch-a-Sketch board for my sins, with a few quick shakes the problem was erased? God is looking for a broken and contrite heart.

Day 95
Stupid Criminals (Psalm 52)

I must admit, I love stupid criminal stories. You know those stories. They are about criminals who are convinced they will never get caught, but they do stupid things in their pride that end up getting them caught.

I loved the story of the guy who broke into a house while a family was on vacation, but he got himself locked in the garage. He had to eat dog food for several days. When the family came home, there he was. Then there was the criminal who broke into a home. He used a folded piece of mail to shimmy into the sliding glass door lock. He stole a ton of stuff. He was quickly apprehended because when he left, he left behind the piece of mail. It was his own mail, complete with his name and address. Oh, and then there are the countless stupid criminals who steal stuff and then post about it on social media, bragging about all their new things. Some even post videos! It is like a video confession just sitting there for the authorities. Stupid criminals crack me up.

Here is the truth: We are all stupid criminals if we think we can get away with sin. It is only because God is good and merciful that we do not immediately pay the repercussions of our actions and choices.

Psalm 52:1 "Why boastest thou thyself in mischief, O mighty man? the goodness of God endureth continually."

Psalm 52 is about a stupid criminal. He loves his sin and mischief. He boasts in it. What he fails to see is that God has him on surveillance camera. God is seeing it all. The criminal will face judgment, but this criminal trusts in his own strength, wisdom, cunning, and riches.

Psalm 52:7 "Lo, this is the man that made not God his strength; but trusted in the abundance of his riches, and strengthened himself in his wickedness."

When a criminal gets caught and pays for his crimes, it sends a message to others to think twice about following his path.

Psalm 52:6 "The righteous also shall see, and fear, and shall laugh at him:"

The righteous see what happens to those who flaunt their sin. The righteous choose to fear instead of follow. They choose to learn the lesson from other person's mistakes instead of having to learn them from their own stupidity. Then the righteous laugh-- they share "stupid criminal" stories because they know that nothing escapes God's view. They think, "Wow! I am not going to do that! God sees everything!"

The moral of this story: Do not be a stupid criminal. God sees. It is like leaving our name and address at the scene of the crime, and we might as well post a video confession because God already knows!

Galatians 6:7 "Be not deceived; God is not mocked: for whatsoever a man soweth, that shall he also reap."

Day 95
Happy April Fool's Day? Oh Dear (Psalm 53)

It happens every year. April 1st rolls around, and as it approaches, my youngest child makes big plans of jokes he will play on that day. We have told him of grand adventures his Daddy and I used to have when his we played April Fool's Day jokes. Daddy has warned him that Mommy is a masterful April Fool's Day prankster and that he should not ever get in an April Fool's Day war with me. My husband is speaking from experience and can tell stories of his wounded pride as he fell victim to my pranks. He and I have agreed on a truce and have not played jokes on each other for many years. He conceded to my superior April Fool's Day skills.

When the day finally rolls around, my youngest child usually has forgotten his evil April Fool's Day plans. The day passes uncelebrated until it is too far spent. The only acknowledgement of the day is found on social media. As I scroll through posts from many friends and family I often see the same words: "Happy Atheist's Day!" This is always followed undoubtedly by part of a verse.

Psalm 53:1 "The fool hath said in his heart, There is no God..."

Since an atheist declares there is no God, many Christians have deemed April Fool's Day as Atheist's Day. Oh, I do agree that an atheist is a fool. It is hard to comprehend someone looking at the organization and beauty of creation and them still be convinced that we arrived as an accident of chemical reactions. Quite foolish indeed! But the rest of the Psalm has something to say about us all. It brings every man, woman, and child under the banner of fool.

> *Psalm 53:3 "Every one of them is gone back: they are altogether become filthy; there is none that doeth good, no, not one."*

The rest of the Psalm declares that we are all fools because there is none righteous. There is none that seeks after God. Before salvation, we are all fools drowning in our own filth of sin and tainted self-righteousness. What about after salvation?

Every time I operate my life without regard to God's Word or His will, I am saying in my heart, "There is no God that I need to seek," I am a fool!

Every time I cover my sin I am declaring in my heart, "There is no God that I will answer to," I am a fool!

Every time I neglect prayer or Bible reading or church attendance, I am announcing proudly, "There is no God that I need to learn from," I am a fool!

When I operate my life independently of my Creator, that is when I have revealed what is truly in my heart. That is when I am saying, "There is no God!"

April Fool's Day is not just "Atheist's Day." It is a reminder to me that my heart is deceitful and desperately wicked, too. Maybe we should say, "Happy We-All-Need-the-Lord Day" because we are all fools.

Day 97
God's Man (Psalm 54:4-5)

I live with him. He really is just an average guy. (Well I think he is pretty special!) My husband is a typical male. He struggles finding things, loves tools and big engines, tinkers with projects in a storage room/workshop, and whines a lot when he is sick. See? He is just an average guy.

Most pastors and missionaries are just average people. If you met them, you would realize that they are not super Christians. My former pastor used to say he was going to write a book called "Pastors are People, Too!" and they are.

There is one thing about these men that is special: They have the call of God on their lives. God has separated them and called them for a special purpose. That is why God blesses those who honor His man, and He rewards evil to those who set themselves against His man. It is not that the man is special. It is that God's calling upon the man is special.

> Psalm 54:4-5 "Behold, God is mine helper: the Lord is with them that uphold my soul. He shall reward evil unto mine enemies: cut them off in thy truth."

David was not a pastor or missionary, but he was God's man, set aside for a special purpose. Even David recognized that God rewards us according to how we treat His man. When Saul was king, David refused to do Saul harm. Saul was trying to kill David, but David would not lift his sword against Saul, because Saul was God's chosen vessel. He was set apart by God for a special purpose.

How do you treat your pastor? How do you treat missionaries? How do you treat preachers? If your husband is one of these, do you remember to treat your husband as God's man? Do you talk bad about men of God? Do you cause them harm? God will reward us according to our treatment of those He has set apart for a special purpose.

Here is something that might ruffle some feathers: How do you treat the President? Do you realize that the President is set apart for a special purpose? It does not matter if a person likes the President or not, God has established him as the leader of the country. His office given to him by God deserves respect.

God has a special purpose for each president. We do not have to agree with the man, but just like David did for Saul, we should not lift our sword nor our tongue against him with disrespect. How do you speak of the President? Is it with respect to his office? Do you pray for these men?

Day 98
It Hurts! (Psalm 54:6)

It has been an emotional day. It is hard to explain, but sometimes the sacrifice is more keenly felt than at other times.

Today my oldest child hopped on a bus and headed to Army Basic Training. It is not that we had to say our goodbyes. We are on the other side of the globe from him already. We said our goodbyes months ago when we left him Stateside as we returned to the field. Today is different though. Today I am reminded that I cannot be there for these big events. Today I did not get to help him pack. I did not get to nag him about running late. I did not get to fix his last good breakfast. I did not get to go with him to the bus station, because God has us in a distant land serving Him.

There are some Christians who say that serving the Lord is never a sacrifice. Maybe those who believe that are stronger Christians than I am. I think maybe they do not understand what the difference between a gift and a sacrifice is. I think maybe that they do not understand that it is okay to sacrifice and that sacrificing is not a sign of spiritual immaturity. I think they do not fully understand what it means to be a "living sacrifice" (Romans 12:1) and what it means to give the "sacrifice of praise" (Jeremiah 33:11; Hebrews 13:15).

I do not think I grasped the meaning of sacrifice until we came to the field. The people here taught me the real meaning of sacrifice. Many times we have been invited to someone's home for a meal. We arrived at their home for the meal. The home was often little more than a shack. Many times it had dirt floors and often only one or two rooms. We sat on the floor or a bed because there was no table or chairs. Then the family fed us a huge meal including meat. We knew this was more than they could afford and that they would feed us until we were full, even if it meant they would go hungry.

They would always serve us first to make sure they had prepared enough to fill us. Sometimes a family would not eat with us for fear of not having enough, and other times it was because they did not have enough plates to serve everyone at the same time. The people were so happy to feed us and serve us. They were not standing there hoping we would only eat a little. They did not have worried looks on their faces wondering if they would get to eat. Yet if we ate too much they would go hungry.

A gift is something you freely give. It costs you something. A sacrifice goes deeper. A sacrifice costs you something precious and valuable. It hurts. It causes a loss. Like hunger pains in the night because you gave your food away, sometimes there are pains in the heart because you gave something more precious than food away.

Does it make a missionary less spiritual because they cry when they feel the sacrifice? Actually, it makes the sacrifice more precious in our Father's eyes. When we shed the tears and still willingly lay the sacrifice on the altar, we declare, "Lord, it hurts, but you are more precious to me than this very precious thing!" He is not looking for dry eyes and pasted on smiles as we offer our sacrifices. He is looking for a willing heart that does not begrudge the sacrifice even when it hurts. He wants us to freely (willingly and liberally) sacrifice.

Psalm 54:6 "I will freely sacrifice unto thee: I will praise thy name, O LORD; for it is good."

Yes, today I feel the heart hunger pains. Today I had to reexamine my heart to make sure that I was still freely sacrificing. Today I had to remind myself just how worthy He is of my praise and my sacrifice. He is worthy of this and much, much more.

Go ahead. Shed the tears. It does not make you less Christian, less spiritual, or less holy, but remember the sacrifice He made for you. Through the pain, through the tears, and through the hurt, He still laid His life down on the altar because you were precious to Him. You were more precious to Him than His own life and all the comforts and glories of Heaven. Take your sacrifice, lay it on the altar, shed the tears, and then say with your whole heart, "You are worthy, Lord."

Today it hurt, but I can honestly say He is worth it.

Day 99
The Great Escape (Psalm 55)

Have you ever seen those escape rooms? I really want to do one of those! They do not have them here, but maybe when we visit the States again we can try one. Escape rooms are rooms filled with puzzles and gadgets that you and your team have to solve in order to unlock the door and get out of the room. That sounds like so much fun!

Last year I hosted a July Fourth party at our house. I set up three mini escape rooms for three teams. They had to solve the puzzles in order to unlock a door. I had almost as much fun setting that up as I would have if I were a participant.

Here is the thing about escape rooms: you have to solve the puzzles before you can escape.

> Psalm 55:6-8 "And I said, Oh that I had wings like a dove! for then would I fly away, and be at rest. Lo, then would I wander far off, and remain in the wilderness. Selah. I would hasten my escape from the windy storm and tempest."

David had a problem. This problem sent him into emotional turmoil. He was struggling! He spoke of his heart being "sore pained", of terrors of death, fearfulness, and trembling. He wanted to escape! He wanted the wings of a dove, and he wanted to fly away from his problems.

We do the same thing. We often default to escape plans rather than dealing with our problems in a Godly and Biblical way. We use mechanisms to unplug and distract us from the issue at hand. Whether it be jumping on social media for hours, watching television, reading a book, shopping, getting together with friends-- these can all be escape tools. They are escapes from reality. Some of these things may not be bad things themselves, but when we use them to avoid dealing with or thinking about our problems they become destructive behaviors. When these things are used to mask and to relieve painful emotions so that we do not have to deal with them, they are not healthy choices.

In order to escape the escape room, we must deal with the problems. We must face the problems and seek the Lord for help.

> Psalm 55:1 "Give ear to my prayer, O God; and hide not thyself from my supplication."

The solution is to go to the Problem Solver and His precious Word.

> Psalm 55:16-17 "As for me, I will call upon God; and the LORD shall save me. Evening, and morning, and at noon, will I pray, and cry aloud: and he shall hear my voice."

Day 100
Butter Lips (Psalm 55:12-13)

We live in a country where persecution is real. Spiritual oppression is constant, and the battle is exhausting. We have become accustomed to being vigilant and watching for the enemy. He is tricky and relentless. He desires to sift us. He battles for our minds. He battles for our testimonies. He battles for our time and our desires. We do our best not to let our guard down.

There are people in this country who are against us being here. They try to trap Christians in their words, seek to have foreigners deported, and desire to cause trouble for the church in any way they can. Those are the enemies that surround us. They do not surprise us. We know they are against us.

Then there is another enemy. This enemy seems to catch us off guard. This enemy comes from a direction that is unexpected. This enemy has buttery smooth words. This enemy eats at our table. This enemy laughs with us, and we counsel them and cry with them. They sit beside us in church or maybe even in our own home. This enemy slithers in under the cloak of friendship, and we never see the attack coming. We give our trust and our affection to them, and then they strike. It leaves us reeling. David knew this kind of enemy.

Psalm 55:12-13 "For it was not an enemy that reproached me; then I could have borne it: neither was it he that hated me

that did magnify himself against me;
then I would have hid myself from
him: But it was thou, a man mine equal,
my guide, and mine acquaintance."

If it were the obvious enemy, David said he could have handled it. He would have expected it. He was prepared for it. This attack came a direction he did not expect. This enemy's attack hurts more and cuts deeper. It leaves wounds and sometimes scars. David left his heart unguarded and gave his friendship and affection freely. He was rewarded with deception and injury.

What do we do when that happens? Do we guard our hearts from injury by refusing to trust people? Do we withhold affection and friendship? Do we learn to be cold and distant? David has a different solution.

Psalm 55:22 "Cast thy burden upon the
LORD, and he shall sustain thee: he shall
never suffer the righteous to be moved."

When it hurts, cast the pain to the Lord. When it cuts, cast it to the Father. He will sustain you. He will heal the hurt. He will strengthen you. Keep loving and reaching out. It will leave you vulnerable sometimes, but God is there to heal your heart.

Day 101
Weekend Warrior (Psalm 56)

We love bicycling. Our family enjoys rocky downhills, windy uphills, and fast roads. My daughter and older son enjoy trail riding. My younger son loves speeding down smooth roads and jumping over bumps. Sometimes we pass other people on bikes. We smile at them and they smile back. It is like we are part of a team, part of a family. Then there are some people we pass on bikes and we immediately know they are what we call "Weekend Warriors."

Weekend Warrior: Someone who does not practice their skill or sport frequently (often only on weekends), and therefore does not improve quickly in fitness and endurance.

They are pretty easy to spot. Often, they have on the wrong gear or they have the wrong bikes for the task. The easiest way to spot the Weekend Warrior, though, is they are pushing their bikes instead of riding them up simple, short inclines. We are certainly happy these Weekend Warriors are getting out there at all, but it is easy to see that the lack of repetition and practice holds them back from progress.

*Psalm 56:1-2 "Be merciful unto me, O God: for man would swallow me up; he fighting **daily** oppresseth me. Mine enemies would **daily** swallow me up: for they be many that fight against me, O thou most High... **Every day** they wrest*

my words: all their thoughts are against
me for evil."

Do you know how frequently the enemy gets out there practicing his sport? Daily! Every day our enemy is practicing his skill. Every single day he is actively seeking whom he may devour. He is no Weekend Warrior. He is a lion who never stops.

What about us? Are we Weekend Warriors? Do we only get in God's Word and under the preaching of the Bible on weekends? Do we only study once a week? Do we neglect Bible time throughout the week? It is no wonder we find ourselves struggling when we are in an uphill battle. We have no endurance and we are ill prepared. If our enemy is daily practicing his trade, should not we also practice our skills in God's Word just as frequently?

The steep uphill climbs and battles will come, but if we have been exercising in the Word, we will be ready.

Just as we see bikers walking and pushing their bikes uphill and can tell they are Weekend Warriors, there is no hiding your Weekend Warrior status when you are struggling over simple inclines. More experienced and prepared "bikers" will still cheer you on and encourage you, but they will also tell you that getting in the Word daily will help you be better prepared for those hills.

Are you a Weekend Warrior?

Day 102
Fix It (Psalm 57)

The storm is raging.
The wind is howling.
The enemy is encompassing...
Yet my heart is fixed.

My eyes are overwhelmed.
My ears are bombarded.
My hands are trembling...
Yet my heart is fixed.

My feet are stumbling.
My knees are knocking.
My legs are weakening...
Yet my heart is fixed.

Fear wants to grip me.
Panic wants to take me.
Darkness tries to break me...
But my heart is fixed.

Under His wings I will hide,
Staying close by His side.
Unto Him will I cry...
Because my heart is fixed.

My foundation is firm,
My step is sure,
My path is clear...
Oh, my heart is fixed!

Peace in the fight,
Songs in the night,
Giving praise is my delight...
Yes, my heart is fixed.

This is my victory.
I did not faint in adversity.
He rescued me and now I sing...
My heart was fixed!

Fixed: fastened upon, focused

> *Psalm 57:7 "My heart is fixed, O God, my heart is fixed: I will sing and give praise."*

Are you facing a battle? Fix your heart (your affections, desires, delights) upon Him. Fasten your heart to Him. Praise Him. Adore Him. Get your eyes off the battle and onto your dearest Love. He will carry you through.

Day 103
Coyote (Psalm 58)

As a little girl, I used to love Saturday morning cartoons. I loved Garfield with all his sarcasm. I loved Tiny Toons. I loved Tom and Jerry. One of my favorite Saturday cartoons was always the iconic Bugs Bunny. I loved watching Bugs outsmart Elmer Fudd, and I loved Foghorn Leghorn trying to teach the chicken hawk boy about hunting chickens.

One of my favorite characters was Wile E. Coyote. Usually he was up against the Road Runner, but occasionally he was after sheep in the pasture. There was a sheep dog watching the sheep. Sometimes the coyote would dress up as a sheep and try to blend in, but the sheep dog always caught him.

How did the sheep dog always know it was the coyote and not a sheep? No matter what the coyote was wearing on the outside, he was still the same coyote on the inside. The same coyote "talk" and sounds, the same coyote smells, the same coyote habits and appetites.

Psalm 58:1-2 "Do ye indeed speak
righteousness, O congregation? do ye
judge uprightly, O ye sons of men? Yea,
in heart ye work wickedness; ye weigh
the violence of your hands in the earth."

Sometimes coyotes come in the church and try to look like sheep, but sooner or later, their coyote "talk," habits, and appetites show themselves. God cannot be fooled even for a second, but sometimes the sheep are fooled for a little while.

There was one thing I never remember seeing on the cartoon, though. I do not think there was an episode that I watched where the sheep dressed up like coyotes. Sadly, in our churches today the sheep slip into coyote costumes, and it makes you wonder if they are sheep. We cannot see the hearts of men, but when their actions and words scream "coyote" it is best for sheep to keep a close eye on them. They may not be sheep at all, and they may be sheep who are still trying to act like coyotes. They have forgotten they are new creatures in Christ. Maybe it is you who has forgotten.

2 Corinthian 5:17 "Therefore if any man be in Christ, he is a new creature: old things are passed away; behold, all things are become new."

If you are saved, you are a sheep. Your conversation (lifestyle) should look like a sheep. In Psalm 58, David speaks to the congregation. They are speaking righteousness, but their hearts and their actions declare coyote. It should concern you that others can see your coyote costume. Even more so, it should make you fear knowing that God sees your heart.

God rewards those who are sheep and act like sheep. He knows who is only dressed up like a sheep.

*Psalm 58:11 "So that a man shall say,
Verily there is a reward for the righteous:
verily he is a God that judgeth in the
earth."*

Day 104
Backed in a Corner (Psalm 59)

One evening when I was younger, my mom and I looked out of the window in our house. Across the way, down a hill and back up another incline, we saw a house on fire. It was blazing! Flames poured out of the front of the house. We knew who lived there and that the situation was serious. They were older and struggled with mobility. Their chance of escape was limited. We were petrified!

My mom grabbed the phone and dialed 911. Within moments, the fire department barreled in with sirens blaring. They arrived on the scene to find my grandfather and a couple of other people burning brush on the far side of the house. The house was not on fire at all, but from our limited perspective the fire looked like it was coming from the house. Our fears were unfounded, and we caused a lot of heartache for several people simply because our perspective was limited.

David had some of those "limited perspective" moments. He was backed into a corner by his enemies. He was trapped. When a person is backed into a corner, their vision is limited. They cannot see the full picture. David was frustrated and at the end of himself. He called out to God, but it seemed like God was not doing anything. He felt alone and forsaken. Then he said it. Actually, he said it twice!

Psalm 59:4-5 "They run and prepare themselves without my fault: awake to

help me, and behold. Thou therefore, O
LORD God of hosts, the God of Israel,
awake to visit all the heathen: be not
merciful to any wicked transgressors.
Selah."

Awake? Was God asleep? Had God accidentally dozed off and forgotten about David? Did God get tired and have to take a siesta?

Psalm 121:3-4 "He will not suffer thy foot
to be moved: he that keepeth thee will
not slumber. Behold, he that keepeth
Israel shall neither slumber nor sleep."

In the country where we live, people ring bells to wake up their gods. Every time I hear those bells, I am thankful that we serve the God who never slumbers nor sleeps. David knew that God does not sleep. He was backed in a corner, felt alone, and it felt like God had forgotten him. It felt like God was sleeping and not taking action. The whole time, God was on the throne, wide awake, and still in control.

God is never backed into a corner. He never loses sight of the full picture. His vision is never impaired or limited. He knows when it is the best time to respond. He knows exactly what to do and when to do it. Just because He is not moving when and how we want does not mean He is sleeping. Remember Lazarus? He was dead four days. Martha and Mary were convinced Jesus arrived late. In all actuality, He was perfectly timed.

When Jesus took on a physical body, His physical body needed rest, but He was never unplugged. He never woke from His sleep groggy and disoriented, unaware of what had happened while His physical body refreshed through sleep. He was still 100% God at all times even though He was also 100% man.

When he was asleep on the boat and a storm came, He was still in control. When they woke His physical body, He was not startled by a storm. He could sleep physically through the storm, because He was still completely aware and in control.

When you feel backed into a corner and you feel like God is sleeping in your greatest hour of need, remember that we serve the living God who never sleeps, never takes a day off, never tires, and is not bound by our physical limitations. Do not panic. He is still in control.

Day 105
I Have Been Flagged! (Psalm 60)

I cannot hide it. I am a pretty patriotic person. I love hosting the July Fourth annual party for fellow laborers in this country. I love decorating in red, white, and blue. I love displaying the American flag. It means something special to me.

One year, I hosted a homeschool day, and it was about the American flag: what it means, the history, and flag protocol. It was a great day of projects, games, and hands-on learning. I taught the group of homeschool students how to properly fold the flag. The Stars and Stripes still mean something special to me even though I live in a new country.

Flags (banners) mean something. They can be used to represent a group. They can be used to communicate. They can be used to declare a status or situation.

> *Psalm 60:3-4 "Thou hast shewed thy people hard things: thou hast made us to drink the wine of astonishment. Thou hast given a banner to them that fear thee, that it may be displayed because of the truth. Selah."*

In Psalm 60, David describes a difficult situation. In the beginning of the Psalm, David explains that God was chastising His people. They had turned their backs on Him, and God responded with severe discipline. It was painful and costly. The things that God did left the children of Israel standing in awe and astonishment. They were hard things!

Then David switches gears and talks about a banner (flag) that is displayed because of truth. What does that have to do with this battle and chastisement? It will make more sense if you see the other flag in this Psalm.

> *Psalm 60:1 "O God, thou hast cast us off, thou hast scattered us, thou hast been displeased; O turn thyself to us again."*

There is a white flag of surrender. David hoists this flag high in fear and reverence to his God. His flag of surrender declares, "You are right, Lord. We deserve this. Our sin has earned this. Please have mercy and turn Thyself to us again!"

As David humbled himself, his banner of surrender turned into a banner of victory and truth. Those who fear the Lord hold this banner high. It is a banner that declares God's holiness that must judge sin. It is a banner that declares God's mercy that reaches out to man. It is a banner that declares God is true to His Word and that His Word is true. It is a beautiful banner that is precious to those who know the Lord and treasure His character and nature. They fear Him and love Him. We can all carry this banner, but only if we first hoist the banner of surrender and repentance when we realize we have sinned against our God.

Day 106
Avalanche! (Psalm 61)

A mountain-high to-do list,
Cooking, cleaning, shopping, grading, mopping,
I am overwhelmed.

A schedule towers over me.
A wedding, traveling, appointments, commitments,
I am overwhelmed.

The language barrier casts a cold shadow over me,
Classes, studying, writing practice, listening,
speaking, stuttering, stammering,
I am overwhelmed.

Ministry hovers over me.
Preparing, teaching, cutting, planning,
I am overwhelmed.

The avalanche begins its descent.
Toppling. Rumbling. Threatening. Pursuing.
I call out.

> *Psalm 61:2 "From the end of the earth*
> *will I cry unto thee, when my heart is*
> *overwhelmed: lead me to the rock that is*
> *higher than I."*

He hears. He is there.
His wings to cover me,
A Tower to lift me,
A Shelter to protect me.

A Rock to hide me.
I am safe in the Rock that is higher than I.

Above the avalanche of worries and woes.
No longer overwhelmed.
Now overjoyed.
Praises pouring forth.

Psalm 61:8 "So will I sing praise unto thy name for ever, that I may daily perform my vows."

Day 107
Only and All Times (Psalm 62)

An untested faith is an unreliable faith.

It is easy to say we trust the Lord completely, but when we are put through the heat of trials the true depth of our faith will be revealed. David knew about the refining and revealing nature of trials. He gave two main declarations:

1) Trust only in the Lord.

Three times in this Psalm, David uses the word "only" in reference to God.

> Psalm 62:2 "He only is my rock and my salvation; he is my defence; I shall not be greatly moved."

> Psalm 62:5-6 "My soul, wait thou only upon God; for my expectation is from him. He only is my rock and my salvation: he is my defence; I shall not be moved."

Wait only upon God. He only is my rock.

We declare we completely trust Him, but when trials come, what do our actions, attitudes, and words say we trust? David said there was a temptation to trust in other things.

*Psalm 62:10 "Trust not in oppression,
and become not vain in robbery: if riches
increase, set not your heart upon them."*

Oppression: strength, "strong-arming" your problems, control

When a trial comes along, do you depend on inner strength, fortitude, or positive attitude and nature? Do you trust your talents or skills? Do not trust in how you can control (oppress) the situation. David was tempted in this area. As king, he had access to a great army. He had amazing resources at his disposal, and yet he chose to trust in his God.

Robbery: Taking something that is not yours.

When a trial comes your way, do you resort to things that are off-limits to Christians? Do you scheme and plot? Do you try to use your own logic to solve the problem instead of following the lead of the Spirit and God's Word? Sometimes God has a plan that does not make sense logically. He sometimes tells us "no" to things that are not necessarily sin. They just are not His will for us. When we try to go down a path that God says no to, it is like robbery. That is not our path to take.

Riches: Financial security, assets, and resources. House, job, bank account, car, health, etc.

When trials come, is your confidence in your resources? Do you think your job is secure? Do you think your home is safe? If God allows these things to be taken away, will your faith be shaken? Will you be consumed with depression? Will you still serve Him if your health is taken from you?

2) Trust in Him at all times, good and bad!

> *Psalm 62:8 "Trust in him at all times; ye*
> *people, pour out your heart before him:*
> *God is a refuge for us. Selah."*

It is so easy to praise Him and trust Him when things go smoothly, but the real test begins when things are not easy or comfortable. David said to trust Him at all times. He said to learn to make calling out to Him your first resort and your battle plan for when trials come instead of relying on your strength, logic, or financial stability.

What do you do when trials come? When the next trial hits, take note of what you default to in order to solve the problem.

Day 108
Shooting Arrows (Psalm 64)

Our family certainly is adventurous. We love trying new things like mountain biking, rock climbing, snorkeling, and white-water rafting. My husband and the older boy even went paragliding. The rest of us are wanting in on some of that action!

One of the surprising activities available here is archery. I loved it from the first time I went. We went in a large room. There were several targets posted on a wall across the room. On the near side of the room there was a line on the floor. We were not allowed to cross that line while shooting was taking place. We had to shoot at the targets from a distance. That is the nature of bows and arrows. They must be shot from a distance.

Psalm 64:2-4 "Hide me from the secret counsel of the wicked; from the insurrection of the workers of iniquity: Who whet their tongue like a sword, and bend their bows to shoot their arrows, even bitter words: That they may shoot in secret at the perfect: suddenly do they shoot at him, and fear not."

The wicked aim at their targets from a distance. They sharpen their tongues and words, and they speak in secret. Like an archer who keeps his distance for safety, these people make sure they are not close to those who they want to hit when they release their weapons.

Have you ever had an attack like that? Have you ever listened to an attack upon someone else? Have you ever been guilty of shooting verbal arrows at someone from a distance?

Gossip is no laughing matter. Slander is an evil practice. God does not look lightly upon those who use their tongues as weapons.

Psalm 64:7 "But God shall shoot at them with an arrow; suddenly shall they be wounded."

God also has words that are weapons. His Word is sharp and cutting.

Hebrews 4:12 "For the word of God is quick, and powerful, and sharper than any twoedged sword, piercing even to the dividing asunder of soul and spirit, and of the joints and marrow, and is a discerner of the thoughts and intents of the heart."

God's Word is true, and it hits right to the heart. His Words hit their target every time. He will defend the upright.

1) If someone shoots arrows of gossip or slander your direction, trust the Lord to fight the battle for you. Do

not be afraid of the arrows of the wicked. Instead trust in the arrows of the Lord.

> *Psalm 64:1-2 "Hear my voice, O God, in my prayer: preserve my life from fear of the enemy. Hide me from the secret counsel of the wicked; from the insurrection of the workers of iniquity:"*

2) If someone approaches you to shoot arrows at someone else, put a stop to it. Do not take part in their wickedness.

> *Proverbs 20:19 "He that goeth about as a talebearer revealeth secrets: therefore meddle not with him that flattereth with his lips."*

3) If you are shooting arrows at someone, being a talebearer or a gossip, stop it! You are behaving like the wicked!

> *Proverbs 6:16-19 "These six things doth the LORD hate: yea, seven are an abomination unto him: A proud look, a lying tongue, and hands that shed innocent blood, An heart that deviseth wicked imaginations, feet that be swift in running to mischief, A false witness that speaketh lies, and he that soweth discord among brethren."*

Day 109
Praise Transformation (Psalm 66)

I love watching my children grow. They transform from these tiny non-waking humans who need diapers and need someone to feed them into independent adults. I remember my oldest child when he was little. He was the cutest little boy you ever saw! Now he is a grown man in the Army. My younger son is just about to hit his main growth spurt. Just as his older brother changed before my eyes, I am witnessing it happen all over again.

In our Christian lives, there are many areas that grow and develop as we mature spiritually. When I read Psalm 66, I was confronted with one area of my Christian life that still seems to be in its infancy stage. I thought I was doing well, but as I dig in God's Word, the Spirit is revealing the truth of where I am. What area is lagging behind in its growth?

Psalm 66:2 "Sing forth the honour of his name: make his praise glorious."

This last year or two, I began dabbling in cake decorating. At first, I made cakes that were quite hideous, but they were colorful and creative. As a friend took me under her wing to teach me a few things, my cake skills blossomed a little more. My cakes became at least photo worthy. Now I am no expert, but I no longer blush at my attempts.

I have a friend online that is a professional cake decorator. He makes elaborate cakes that are magazine-worthy. They truly are glorious to behold. They are worthy of being presented before a bride and groom or for a milestone birthday or anniversary.

As I read Psalm 66, I am struck by the phrase "make his praise glorious". When I look at my praise to my God and my Saviour, I think my praise more resembles my first attempts at cake decorating. It is not very beautiful, though it comes from a heart that desires to worship. Just as my cakes tasted good in spite of their appearance, my praise even in its infancy stage makes my Father smile. He is pleased, but He is worthy of glorious praise.

Even more than I desire to develop as a cake decorator, I desire my praise to grow and be fit for the wonderful Saviour and Lord that He is. Just as I needed my friend to teach me cake decorating, I need God to teach me how to praise. Psalm 66 is a great place to start.

How do we make His praise glorious?

1. Learn to praise directly to God (vs 3) and praise Him before man (vs 5, 16)
2. Learn to praise Him when I am alone (vs 16-17) and learn to praise Him with others (vs 4, 5, 8)
3. Learn to praise Him for future things (vs 3, 4), for present things (vs 5, 7), and for past things (vs 6)
4. Learn to praise Him in singing (vs 2, 4), in speaking (vs 3), and in shouting (vs 17, extol means praise enthusiastically)
5. Learn to praise Him in good times (vs 6) and in hard times (vs 10-12)

6. Learn to praise Him joyfully (vs 1), faithfully (vs 13-14), thankfully (vs 8), sacrificially (vs 13, 15), and righteously (vs 18)
7. Learn to praise Him for who He is (vs 2, 3, 7, 8, 18, 20) and for what He does (vs 3, 5, 6, 9, 10-12, 19)

I have many times had my children bring me something they made for me out of love that did not look very beautiful. I smiled and accepted it because I know they did their best. Their "cakes" were precious to me. I often picture my praise before the Father being the same way. As pitiful as it looks, He smiles at me and accepts it. As I grow as a Christian, though, I want to learn to make His praise glorious. He is worthy of the best, and so much more.

Day 110
The Funnel of Love (Psalm 67)

You know what the difference between a funnel and a bowl is? It seems pretty obvious. One has a hole in it and the other does not. One captures and keeps everything, and the other directs everything to a different location. Both are blessed recipients of things, but only one willingly "spreads the love."

> Psalm 67:1-2 "To the chief Musician on Neginoth, A Psalm or Song. God be merciful unto us, and bless us; and cause his face to shine upon us; Selah. That thy way may be known upon earth, thy saving health among all nations."

The Psalmist was praying for God's mercy and blessing. He wanted God's face to shine upon his people. Was it so they could hoard the blessings? Was it so they could show off to the world how blessed and awesome they were, or so they could get so much stuff that they had to build bigger barns to store it all?

According to verse 2, he wanted God to pour on the blessings so that the world would know the one true God, His goodness, and His salvation. He wanted the whole world to praise the LORD. For the psalmist, God's blessings were not about him and his people gathering great bounty like a bowl, but it was about being a funnel. He knew the blessings of God in his life could impact the lives of others.

What does this mean for us today? How does this apply in modern times? You know that blessing you received recently? Did you pocket it, or did you seek for some way to use it for God's glory and to reach others with the Gospel? That income tax refund you are expecting, are you pretty excited to buy a new gadget or toy, or are you seeking how you may invest in eternity? That paycheck you receive, do you spend it selfishly serving all your own needs, or do you give tithes, offerings, and missions money? Do you help those in need?

If God has your heart, He will have no problem having your pocket book. Your eyes will be focused on eternity and the trinkets of this world will not have the glimmer and sparkle they once had. You will learn to be a funnel instead of a bowl, because you will realize how temporary things are on this earth. Eternity matters forever.

Luke 12:34 "For where your treasure is, there will your heart be also."

Day 111
Broken (Psalm 68:5-6)

There is a practice in this country that is heartbreaking. Often families are split apart because the husband decides to go off to work in another country, leaving the wife to raise the children alone. Sometimes it is the mother who goes. Even more tragic is when both parents leave the country to work, leaving the children with a grandparent.

These children grow up not really knowing their parents. The parents chase dreams of making a lot of money, when in actuality they end up in worse financial condition than they were in the beginning. In their new country of employment, they are often abused, neglected, and taken advantage of. Some fall for employment schemes that give great promises of money, only to discover they were tricked into being a mule for drugs or illegal goods. Those people end up in prison in their new country.

Their lives are ruined, and the family is torn apart. My heart breaks for the whole family, but even more for the children. You see it in their eyes. The children hunger for love, security, and affection. They hunger for the home to be what God designed it to be, yet none of them knows what is missing in their lives. It is like walking around in darkness, groping for something you do not know is out there.

There is another story, too. Sometimes the fathers/husbands are in the home, but alcohol plagues their existence. Women come into our church toting their small children along. They request prayer for their unbelieving husbands who get drunk and then beat them. No, the husband will not be prosecuted in this culture. Often the family is seen as the father's property. How he wants to tend to his family is his business. You can see the age and the wear on the faces of these women. My heart breaks for them.

Not even half a mile from our home there is a park. Elderly women often walk there. They go to the temple to do their idol worship and then walk in the park to get fresh air and exercise. The story of these women, more often than not, is that they live in a home for widows nearby. They usually have adult children, but these women are neglected and unwanted. Because they are aging, they are cumbersome to the family. If the family can afford it, the family puts these women in a home to get them out of the way. These elderly women are not valued. Sometimes as I talked with these women at the park, tears would well up in their eyes when I asked if they had family.

We live in a broken world. Sin has devastated the home. These people are bound by sin and circumstance. What is the solution? We must give them hope.

> Psalm 68:5-6 "A father of the fatherless,
> and a judge of the widows, is God in his
> holy habitation. God setteth the solitary
> in families: he bringeth out those which
> are bound with chains: but the rebellious
> dwell in a dry land."

Our Saviour, Jesus, is the answer to the longing in their hearts. He can fill the empty gap. He can satisfy their hearts' desires. He is the solution to mend the broken heart and the broken home. A Father to the fatherless, He also takes care of the widow. This world needs Christ whether they realize it or not. I need Christ. You need Him. The things of this world will leave us empty and broken. He, however, satisfies our every need.

Day 112
Push-Ups and Lost Phone Privileges
(Psalm 69)

If anyone knows anything about Basic Training in the Army, they know that push-ups are a way of life. The soldiers in training do push-ups for anything and everything. Contraband items in their possession, taking too long to do something, waking up in the morning... time for more push-ups.

Right now, I am waiting for a phone call from my son in the Army. It is getting late, and I am concerned that his platoon lost phone call privileges this week. I bet if they did, they also had to do push-ups. It is possible that as a group they failed at something, but more often than not they lose privileges because a handful of people got into trouble. When they have to do push-ups or lose phone privileges for another person's stupidity, that is frustrating.

The question then is posed: Why do they all have to pay the price for one or two people's mistakes? Can't the leaders just punish the ones who did wrong?

Of course they could! But then that would be missing out on the valuable lesson. What in the world could a Drill Sergeant be teaching by punishing everyone? The lesson is simple. Our mistakes impact everyone around us. I would rather those soldiers in training learn that lesson over a Twinkie in a footlocker than for an overlooked detail that gets several killed!

> *Psalm 69:5-6 "O God, thou knowest my foolishness; and my sins are not hid from thee. Let not them that wait on thee, O Lord GOD of hosts, be ashamed for my sake: let not those that seek thee be confounded for my sake, O God of Israel."*

David did not want those who were faithful to the Lord to face reproach or to be confused and frustrated because of what he was facing. Not only was David a sinful man, but he was also facing reproach without just cause. His enemies hated him for no good reason. David was facing hardship from them that was undeserved and unjustified.

> *1 Peter 3:14 "But and if ye suffer for righteousness' sake, happy are ye: and be not afraid of their terror, neither be troubled;"*

There are times when we suffer persecution and reproach for righteousness. It should be something we endure happily for Christ. He has a purpose in it. He, too, suffered persecution for righteousness.

What is frustrating is suffering for someone else's sin. Let it always remind us that our own sin always impacts others.

(Update: We got a call just now! Yay! Love that boy!)

Day 113
Going AWOL (Psalm 65)

Everyone here misses our oldest child who moved back to the States and enlisted in the Army. They keep asking about him and how he is doing. One of the questions that they often ask is what would happen if our son decided he did not want to be a soldier anymore. We tell them of the serious consequences of going AWOL (absent without leave). Our son made a commitment to the military for a certain amount of time, and he is obligated to fulfill that commitment.

Psalm 65:1 "Praise waiteth for thee, O God, in Sion: and unto thee shall the vow be performed."

The children of Israel, including David, also made a vow. Their vow was to praise the Lord for His goodness, blessings, and provision. This Psalm goes on to tell of how good God had been to them and how worthy He is of praise.

Do we have a commitment to praise the Lord? We should. He certainly is worthy. We should commit to praising Him every day, and we should take that vow seriously. Too often, though, we are AWOL in our praise. When circumstances are tough or we are tired or our day did not go as we expect, we decide to skip praising the Lord. We take a day or two (or several) off from singing and shouting His praises. He is still faithful and good even on days when we do not feel like praising Him.

One day last week, I saw a picture of my son online. His platoon was doing their physical training (PT) at 5:30 AM in the winter, outside. I bet he was not feeling like being a soldier at that time in the morning, but he manned up and broke a sweat with the rest of his platoon. My boy does not like to be cold, but he made a commitment. Even at 5:30 in the morning he was determined to keep that commitment.

Some days, we are not going to feel like doing our PT (Praise and Thanksgiving). On those days we need to remind ourselves of our commitment and God's worthiness. We need to be sure we do not go AWOL on our worship and praise. God never goes AWOL on His grace and mercy.

Day 114
Searching for my SIT (Psalm 63)

Do not laugh. Okay, you can laugh a little. Honestly, my daughter and I laughed a lot.

Since my son recently went into Army Basic Training, I have been scouring through every photo posted from his battery on the internet. I have not seen my son since July when he returned to the States, so these pictures are priceless to me.

Every morning I get up to see if new pictures are posted of my SIT (Soldier in Training). I go to bed at night thinking about the possibility of pictures being posted. It is my last thought at night and my first thought in the morning. When pictures are finally posted, I go on a "Where's Waldo" adventure, but all these Waldos are wearing the same style of clothes! There is only one difference. Sometimes they are wearing color-coded and numbered jerseys.

About a week ago, the first round of pictures was posted. I spotted him in two pictures. My heart soared! I saved the pictures to my phone. I even put one on my phone as a wallpaper. It was a side shot of him putting on gloves as his platoon was in formation. They were wearing toboggans and his collar covered part of his face, but I would know my son's profile anywhere! The other picture was from a distance and slightly blurry, but he was tall and stood just like my son. Yes, that is my boy!

This week, a new set of pictures was posted. There he was in several pictures. Two of them were close-ups. Definitely my boy! But I noticed his jersey number in these pictures was different than in his other pictures. I thought that was very strange, so I did some research. I asked other Army Moms and wives. They assured me that the soldiers always wear the same jersey number. So, for a week I have had the picture of some stranger's son on my phone thinking it was my kid, I stared at it every chance I got, too.

What a thrill to find the real deal, though. Sometimes we think we know our kids and that we could spot them anywhere. We think we know what they are like. Then we realize we did not know them as well as what we thought we did.

We are like that with the Lord, too. We are convinced we know Him, but then as we get into the Word, we learn what He is really like. Just as my son's real jersey number identifies him without a doubt, the Bible points to the real God so that there is no mistaking who He is and what He is really like.

What if we had the same level of hunger to see Him that I have had for my son? What if He was our first thought in the morning and our last thought at night? What if we went scouring through the Bible daily to seek Him?

Psalm 63:1 "O God, thou art my God;
early will I seek thee: my soul thirsteth
for thee, my flesh longeth for thee in a
dry and thirsty land, where no water is;"

*Psalm 63:6 "When I remember thee upon
my bed, and meditate on thee in the
night watches."*

*Psalm 63:8 "My soul followeth hard after
thee: thy right hand upholdeth me."*

Often, we have imagined in our minds what
God is like, but if we had a hunger and appetite for
Him we would get into the Bible to see what He is
really like. Just as finding the real pictures of my real
son gave me great satisfaction and confidence, so
does getting in the Word give satisfaction and
confidence. We get to know who the Lord really is.

When we have a false view of God in our
minds, it is like having some other mom's son's
picture on your phone. It will make you smile until you
realize that is not your son! Then it will make you feel
quite silly. I could keep that other guy's picture on my
phone and pretend it is my boy, but why do that when
I can have the real deal? Why be satisfied with a
facsimile of God that we have created in our own
minds when we can get in the Word and get the real
picture of who He is?

*Psalm 63:5 "My soul shall be satisfied as
with marrow and fatness; and my mouth
shall praise thee with joyful lips:"*

How hungry are we for the real deal? Are we
satisfied with a fake view of the Lord? Are we hungry
enough to go searching, seeking Him early and daily?
Are we convinced we know Him enough already? We

just might be surprised that our view was wrong all along.

Day 115
Lost Socks (Psalm 70:4)

I have a confession. My biggest pet peeve is when I cannot find something. It drives me crazy to waste time looking for something that is not where it is supposed to be. This is especially frustrating when we are in a hurry to go somewhere. Maybe it is missing keys or a misplaced Bible. Whatever it is, I struggle having a meek and quiet spirit when the minutes tick away as we search the house for an item that should have been put in a specific place but was not.

My family, however, knows that I am the queen of finding things. If it is anywhere in the house, I can find it. I can find it in much less time than anyone else because I know exactly where to look. I know the habits of my family and where they are likely to have absent-mindedly placed something. I ask them a few questions to narrow down the possibilities, and then within minutes the item is in hand. We rejoice and are glad. We celebrate and are once again at peace.

> Psalm 70:4 "Let all those that seek thee rejoice and be glad in thee: and let such as love thy salvation say continually, Let God be magnified."

Do you seek the Lord? He is not misplaced. He was not absent-mindedly left somewhere. He is right where He is supposed to be. When we struggle finding Him, it is because we are looking for Him in the wrong places and in the wrong things. We look for the joy He brings by looking at in people, in circumstances, and in places. We seek Him in places and ways that He declares He will not be found. We develop our own plans, methods, and worldly/fleshly means to attempt conjuring up God. Really those things show us that we are not looking for God. We are instead looking for a deity that lives by our terms and expectations. The true and holy God will only be found on His terms.

Imagine if my youngest child misplaced an item, a sock. I decide to help him find it, so I search for his orange Adidas sock. I look and look. For some reason, I cannot find it. I go to him and tell him I cannot find his orange sport sock.

"Mom, I do not have an orange Adidas sock. I am looking for my red Adidas sock!" No wonder I cannot find his sock!

Searching for God is the same thing. Sometimes we cannot find Him because we are looking for something He is not!

"Well, your red sock is in the drawer where it belongs."

"Oh, I did not look in there." (Sorry to compare the holy Lord to a sock, but I have searched for a lot of socks in my time. The illustration was handy and easy.) Yes, God is always right where He is supposed to be, but if we refuse to look for Him in the places where He is, we will never find Him. If we have misguided notions of what God is like and who He is, we will struggle in our seeking.

Exactly where can we find the Lord? In His Word. His Word describes who He is and what He is like. If you are searching for God in other places, you are wasting your time. If you are searching for God, but not opening the Bible, you are not really seeking Him at all.

Jeremiah 29:13 "And ye shall seek me, and find me, when ye shall search for me with all your heart."

Isaiah 55:6 "Seek ye the LORD while he may be found, call ye upon him while he is near:"

Day 116
Retirement? No Way! (Psalm 71)

Last night, our family had an amazing family devotion time. We traced the children's Godly Christian heritage for them so that they could see how they arrived where they are today. On my side, their heritage starts with me. I did not become a Christian until I was eighteen years old, and I was not raised in a Christian home. I am considered first generation. Much like Timothy's grandmother, it has been my responsibility and privilege to start the line. (Paul traced Timothy's Christian heritage, too.)

> *2 Timothy 1:5 "When I call to remembrance the unfeigned faith that is in thee, which dwelt first in thy grandmother Lois, and thy mother Eunice; and I am persuaded that in thee also."*

On my husband's side, his mother was saved as a teenager, but she did not grow nor pass on her Christian heritage at first. His father was in the Navy and met a friend. That friend invited him to church. My husband's dad accepted Christ as his Saviour. At that time, he was already married to "Gramma," and they had two young children. They had no training, but they began faithfully learning, growing, and teaching their boys the best they could. Because of their faithfulness, my husband heard the Gospel as a child. My husband accepted Christ as a preteen.

In high school, my husband met me and invited me to church. I accepted Christ. We later married and had children. We passed on our Christian heritage to our children. Now the responsibility rests on their shoulders. The question is: "Are you going to continue this Godly Christian heritage, or are you going to drop the ball? Are you going to quit being faithful somewhere along the way?"

David declares, much like our children could declare, that from his youth he was taught and raised to know God.

> Psalm 71:5 "For thou art my hope, O Lord GOD: thou art my trust from my youth."

> Psalm 71:6" By thee have I been holden up from the womb: thou art he that took me out of my mother's bowels: my praise shall be continually of thee."

> Psalm 71:17 "O God, thou hast taught me from my youth: and hitherto have I declared thy wondrous works."

From his youth He dedicated his life to following the Lord. He was taught, and he followed in that teaching. He continued a heritage, but he did not stop there. He continued even farther!

vs 6: "... from the womb... my praise shall be continually of thee."

vs 8, 15: "... all the day."

vs 14: "... hope continually..."

vs 17: "... from my youth: and hitherto..."

He continued on and was faithful, but he did not stop there either. He talked about continuing farther. He hungered for that close relationship to continue his whole life, even when he was gray headed.

> Psalm 71:9 "Cast me not off in the time of old age; forsake me not when my strength faileth."

> Psalm 71:18 "Now also when I am old and grayheaded, O God, forsake me not..."

The most exciting part to me is not that he wanted a close fellowship with God his whole life. It thrills my soul to no end that he also determined and purposed in his heart to serve God even in his old age. He did not have a "retirement" mindset about his Christian heritage and serving God. He was not content to let the young guys take over. He took personal responsibility for reaching the next generation as long as he still had breath.

> Psalm 71:18 "Now also when I am old and gray-headed, O God, forsake me not; until I have shewed thy strength unto this generation, and thy power to every one that is to come."

Just because we grow grey headed and wrinkled, slow or bedridden, does not mean we stop serving. When the body is aging, tired, and weary, how can a person still serve God?

Praise:

> Psalm 71:8 "Let my mouth be filled with thy praise and with thy honour all the day."

This next generation needs to see what real worship and praise is.

Faith:

> Psalm 71:14 "But I will hope continually, and will yet praise thee more and more."

This next generation needs to see faith (hope, confident expectation) lived out in daily life. They need to see someone who lives daily trusting in God's perfect Word, learning and growing in the Word even in old age.

Teach:

> Psalm 71:15 "My mouth shall shew forth thy righteousness and thy salvation all the day; for I know not the numbers thereof."

This next generation still needs to know who God is and what He has done. With a life full of stories of God's provision, protection, and providence, shall we silence those stories because we are old? Shall they not hear of a real saving faith that changed our lives?

Dependence on God:

> Psalm 71:16 "I will go in the strength of the Lord GOD: I will make mention of thy righteousness, even of thine only."

In a world that fills their ears full of lies that the answers are in them and that they are strong, not needing anyone, shall we not in our old age show them the truth? Shall we not tell them that without Christ we can do nothing? Will our faltering bodies silence this truth?

Sing:

> Psalm 71:22 "I will also praise thee with the psaltery, even thy truth, O my God: unto thee will I sing with the harp, O thou Holy One of Israel."

Oh, how our Father loves to hear us sing! The wrinkles on our brow do not distract Him as He bends to hear the singing of His praises. Shall this next generation not be touched by our heart's adoration of the Saviour in song?

Rejoice:

> Psalm 71:23 "My lips shall greatly rejoice when I sing unto thee; and my soul, which thou hast redeemed."

This world is full of complaining, and it seems to be a heritage that is passed on generation to generation. How do we stop it? When we are old and aching and yet we still praise Him, we declare to the next generation that God is good all the time. We spread an attitude of gratitude.

Proclaim:

> Psalm 71:24 "My tongue also shall talk of
> thy righteousness all the day long: for
> they are confounded, for they are
> brought unto shame, that seek my hurt."

No matter how old we get, we can pass on to the next generation the truth of God's righteousness. We can keep proclaiming His Word even on our deathbed, all the day long, and every day, until we draw our last breath. Be committed, by God's grace, to be the one who will pass on a Godly heritage to the next generation. From youth, continually now, and in old age, do not quit.

Day 117
A Prayer for My Son from the Psalm for David's Son (Psalm 72)

My dear son,

I am praying for you.

Just as David had walked the path of being king before his son Solomon, I have walked the path of becoming an adult. I understand what you face during this transition, and it drives me to my knees for you. Much like David prayed for his son, I pray for you today.

I pray that you will be dependent on God, knowing that wisdom and righteousness, right decisions and strength comes from Him. I pray that you will seek Him and that He will give you the wisdom you need. I pray that He will guide you in righteousness and that you will follow.

Psalm 72:1 "Give the king thy judgments, O God, and thy righteousness unto the king's son."

I pray that you are a Godly leader that is not afraid to take a stand for right. I pray that you care about those who have not been as blessed as you.

Psalm 72:2 "He shall judge thy people with righteousness, and thy poor with judgment."

I pray that the big and dangerous obstacles that you face each day (your mountains and your hills) would not cause you to fear. I pray that you would face them confident in the favor of the Lord because you know He is with you. I pray that as you walk in righteousness, He would bless your path through these towering trials.

Psalm 72:3 "The mountains shall bring peace to the people, and the little hills, by righteousness."

I pray that you would be a guardian to those around you in need, and that you would stand up for the weak.

Psalm 72:4 "He shall judge the poor of the people, he shall save the children of the needy, and shall break in pieces the oppressor."

I pray that those that oppose righteousness, that oppress the poor, and that hate the Lord would be gripped in fear because of you when they know that you stand in God's favor.

Psalm 72:5 "They shall fear thee as long as the sun and moon endure, throughout all generations."

I pray that you will be a refreshing rain to those around you who thirst for truth and hope.

Psalm 72:6 "He shall come down like rain
upon the mown grass: as showers that
water the earth."

I pray that those around you would be encouraged to be better Christians (or to accept Christ) because of the example you live, and that their lives would be impacted with peace simply because they know you.

Psalm 72:7 "In his days shall the
righteous flourish; and abundance of
peace so long as the moon endureth."

I pray that God would increase your circle of influence as you glorify Him.

Psalm 72:8 "He shall have dominion also
from sea to sea, and from the river unto
the ends of the earth."

I pray that even your enemies will begin to thirst for truth when they see your God refreshing and watering you while their lives seem dry as the dust.

Psalm 72:9 "They that dwell in the
wilderness shall bow before him; and his
enemies shall lick the dust."

I pray God would give you favor among leaders around you.

Psalm 72:10-11 "The kings of Tarshish
and of the isles shall bring presents: the

kings of Sheba and Seba shall offer
gifts. Yea, all kings shall fall down before
him: all nations shall serve him."

I pray that your heart is full of compassion and not criticism and impatience.

Psalm 72:12-13 "For he shall deliver the
needy when he crieth; the poor also, and
him that hath no helper. He shall spare
the poor and needy, and shall save the
souls of the needy."

I pray that you will have courage to intervene when the weak cannot defend themselves.

Psalm 72:14 "He shall redeem their soul
from deceit and violence: and precious
shall their blood be in his sight."

I pray for God to provide you with the finances you need, the spiritual help you need, and the encouragement you need.

Psalm 72:15 "And he shall live, and to
him shall be given of the gold of Sheba:
prayer also shall be made for him
continually; and daily shall he be
praised."

I pray that the whole earth, for generations to come, will be blessed because of you.

*Psalm 72:17 "His name shall endure for
ever: his name shall be continued as long
as the sun: and men shall be blessed in
him: all nations shall call him blessed."*

I pray that God will be glorified and exalted, not
you or me.

*Psalm 72:18-19 "Blessed be the LORD
God, the God of Israel, who only doeth
wondrous things. And blessed be his
glorious name for ever: and let the whole
earth be filled with his glory; Amen, and
Amen."*

Amen.

Day 118
Falling in a Manhole (Psalm 73)

It matters where my eyes are. When running, if I look around instead of looking forward, there is a good chance I am going to trip. There is also a good chance if I look to the side that I will also veer to the side and get squashed by a vehicle. If I do not look forward, there is even a really good chance I will step in a pile of cow dung from where cows are allowed to wander around anywhere they please. And the ever-beloved open manholes are waiting to swallow up the person who takes her eyes off the road ahead. Yes, running has taught me to look forward and keep my focus on my task.

My son is in Basic Training in the Army. We found out he won a shooting competition in his battery. He has learned how to shoot well. Part of shooting is focusing on the target. When shooting, the rifleman cannot be looking at other shooters. They have to focus on their own target. If their eyes wander even slightly, their aim will be affected. The motto is "Aim Small, Miss Small." In other words, pick a very specific point on the target, and the likelihood of missing the target itself is very minute.

The psalmist Asaph knew this concept well. He learned it the hard way. He was "running his race," but almost slipped because his eyes were in the wrong place.

Psalm 73:1-3 "A Psalm of Asaph. Truly
God is good to Israel, even to such as are

of a clean heart.
But as for me, my feet were almost gone;
my steps had well nigh slipped.
For I was envious at the foolish, when I
saw the prosperity of the wicked."

Asaph got his eyes off on the wicked. He knew God was good. He knew God was just, but he started focusing on the prosperity of the wicked. What happened when his eyes wandered? What happened when his focus was distracted? Much like when I run without focusing on the road in front of me, he stepped in the lie that the wicked were flourishing and successful. He tripped on the deception that they had it better than he did. He was almost swallowed by the open "manhole" of discouragement.

Psalm 73:13-14 "Verily I have cleansed
my heart in vain, and washed my hands
in innocency.
For all the day long have I been plagued,
and chastened every morning."

He started believing that the wicked had it better than he did. He let the thoughts play in his mind that he followed God in vain. "I have wasted my time! I am over here with trials and chastening, while the wicked are living the good life! Why did I bother?"

He believed these things until he went to the sanctuary. Then he was refocused on truth. His eyes were redirected on the target.

*Psalm 73:17 "Until I went into the
sanctuary of God; then understood I their
end."*

In the sanctuary, Asaph was reminded that the wicked have an end. They seemed like they were prospering, but they were on a slippery slope. It was only a matter of time. Asaph, however, was on a firm foundation. Asaph was slipping because he chose to get his eyes off the target, not because he was on slippery ground. When Asaph got in the sanctuary, his thoughts were redirected toward truth. His eyes were refocused on truth.

Why is it so important to go to church? It is a place of refocusing. It is a place where a corporate body of believers get their minds strengthened with truth so that they can keep their eyes focused on the target. That target is glorifying God.

God is good. He has a plan and purpose for every detail in our lives, even the painful and difficult things. If we get our focus on other people, we will forget the goodness of God. We will fall into discouragement. Are you struggling with discouragement? Make sure you are faithfully getting with other believers in church and getting refocused. Purpose to keep your eyes on your goal. Stop looking around at others. Keep your eyes on Him.

*Psalm 73:28 "But it is good for me to
draw near to God: I have put my trust in
the Lord GOD, that I may declare all thy
works."*

Day 119
Tears for Carvings (Psalm 74:5-8)

We stepped into the home. It was not an ordinary home. Most homes are not so grand and do not require a ticket to enter. The splendor was breathtaking. Every corner was decorated. Every wall was adorned. The floor was not neglected in the scenery either. Carpets or expensive tile canvased every place where we would tread. There was not a detail that was overlooked.

As we toured the Biltmore House in Asheville, North Carolina, we were particularly captivated by the elaborate furnishings. The chairs and tables were not merely chairs or tables. They were pieces of artwork. It was clear that every piece of wood was carefully designed and carved by a masterful artist. There were curves, lines, and even floral decorations hand cut by a professional. Oh, the hours of labor and heart that must have gone into every inch of the wood!

Psalm 74:5-8 "A man was famous according as he had lifted up axes upon the thick trees. But now they break down the carved work thereof at once with axes and hammers. They have cast fire into thy sanctuary, they have defiled by casting down the dwelling place of thy name to the ground. They said in their hearts, Let us destroy them together: they have burned up all the synagogues of God in the land."

A man was known for his skill in taking a piece of wood and transforming it into precious art and furnishings. These furnishings captured the eye and the wonderment of those who looked upon the work. And yet how quickly those things can be destroyed. These treasures can be consumed in mere moments, and what tragedy it is when it happens. The pain is keenly felt by those who have experienced the beauty of the work. As the pieces lay scattered across the floor, our hearts would break knowing the time, effort, attention, labor, and heart that went into even one article from the master woodworker. Tears would flow.

God, the Master Designer, has carefully carved and created many things. Two of His most precious designs are the home and the local church. Beautifully and perfectly crafted by the Master, these two items should give us pause and amazement. Often, we pass by them without even glancing at their splendor, but they are fabulous treasures whether we value them or not.

There is a tragedy. The enemy has entered into the sanctuary and has plundered, scratched, and destroyed. Homes are wounded. Local churches are ravaged, and we pass by without a tear.

When is the last time you have shed a tear for the condition of homes and churches? When is the last time you have intensely studied and prepared to care for and protect these precious masterpieces? (Oh, how it must grieve the Master Woodworker to see these treasures ignored, undervalued, neglected, or damaged!)

When is the last time you have studied how the home and the local church are Biblically operated? When is the last time you have focused on fortifying, edifying, and protecting these two masterpieces? How have you invested recently in strengthening the foundations of these treasures?

It is not good enough to simply value these treasures, but we must care for and guard them. They are more priceless and precious than our bubblegum machine trinkets and entertainments.

Day 120
No Horn Zone (Psalm 75)

We live in a noisy city. One of the noisiest things they do is honk their vehicle horns constantly. They honk to let you know they are passing. They honk to let you know they are not stopping. They honk to let you know they are going to pull out in front of you. Sometimes I think they honk just for the fun of it.

They recently passed a law restricting honking. There are "No Horn" zones where you are not allowed to honk at all. In the rest of the city, the rule is only honk for emergency. I bet you are wondering how the law is working.

Well, the city is somewhat quieter. Relatively. Sort of. There is less honking, but that is like saying there are less fish in the ocean because you caught a few. People are addicted to their horns and everyone is used to them. The horn is a simple, yet often annoying, way of saying, "Hey, look at me!"

Have you ever heard the phrase "tooting your own horn"? It comes from the days of heralds when there was a horn blower sent before someone to announce the arrival of someone important. Tooting your own horn is when you arrogantly draw attention to yourself by bragging or boasting. Tooting one's own horn goes farther back in history, too.

In Matthew 6, Jesus taught about people tooting their own horn. When the people would give alms for the poor, sometimes they would blow a trumpet to get people to look and see what they were doing. They wanted people to see how gracious and giving (and rich) they were to give so generously. Then there were those that stood on street corners and prayed out loud so that everyone would hear how spiritual they were. Their own voices became their horns. Jesus said for us to stop tooting our own horns and do things in secret. But the horn thing goes back even farther.

> *Psalm 75:4-7 "I said unto the fools, Deal not foolishly: and to the wicked, Lift not up the horn: Lift not up your horn on high: speak not with a stiff neck. For promotion cometh neither from the east, nor from the west, nor from the south. But God is the judge: he putteth down one, and setteth up another."*

This horn was not one to be tooted or blown. This is talking about an animal horn. Have you ever seen a deer with a huge rack on his head? He regally lifts it up by straightening and stiffening his neck for everyone to see the majestic nature of his stately antlers. His "horns" are his beauty, his power, and his crown. Speaking of crowns, do you know what animal horns were used for in the Old Testament?

> *1 Samuel 16:1 "... fill thine horn with oil, and go, I will send thee to Jesse the Bethlehemite: for I have provided me a king among his sons."*

The horn was filled with oil to anoint the king! It was lifted above the chosen man's head and poured over him. Psalm 75 is saying, "Do not stiffen your neck in pride and lift your own horn of oil over your own head and anoint yourself king!" This passage even declares this attitude, this pride and arrogance, to be the behavior of fools and of the wicked.

And here comes the "ouch".

How often do we do things to be seen? How often do we show off things we have done so that we can receive the praise of people? How often do we post our accomplishments on social media so that people see our beautiful, majestic "horns" on our head?

Let me make it even more personal:

- How often do I share my completed to-do list so that people will see how awesome I am?
- How often do I show off my spiritual opinions and counsel and wisdom so that people will think highly of me?
- How often do I share "How I do it" and set myself up as an example for others to follow?
- How often do I, even in an outward seemingly humble manner, try to exalt myself so that I teach a class, lead a group, lead a devotion time for ladies, etc? (Just being honest!)

If we are in Christ, we live in a "no honking zone". We ought not draw attention to ourselves. We ought not try to volley for position. God is the one who sets up and God is the one who removes leaders. We need to soften our necks and humble our hearts. We need to bow the heart and knee to the real King, the Lord Jesus. We need to stop anointing ourselves, and we need to start pointing to Him.

Galatians 6:14 "But God forbid that I should glory, save in the cross of our Lord Jesus Christ, by whom the world is crucified unto me, and I unto the world."

About the Author

CHARITY WOON serves alongside her husband Jason as independent Baptist missionaries in Southern Asia with Baptist Missions to Forgotten Peoples, Jacksonville, Florida. They are sent out of Woodfin Baptist Church, Asheville, North Carolina, where they served in their local church before God called them to the mission field. They have three children who love adventure as much as they do. They enjoy serving the Lord together as a family.

Charity's books include:

Heart at Home Mom: Focusing the Heart Toward Home in a Career-Minded World

My Princess, Be Pure

Daily in the Depths: A Daily Devotional through the Book of Jonah

The Christmas Critter Character Building Series

Made in the USA
Lexington, KY
08 September 2018